GREEK
TRAGEDIES

VOLUME

1

AESCHYLUS

AGAMEMNON
Translated by Richmond Lattimore

PROMETHEUS BOUND
Translated by David Grene

SOPHOCLES

OEDIPUS THE KING
Translated by David Grene

ANTIGONE
Translated by Elizabeth Wyckoff

EURIPIDES

HIPPOLYTUS
Translated by David Grene

GREEK TRAGEDIES

Edited by

DAVID GRENE *and* RICHMOND LATTIMORE

VOLUME

1

THE UNIVERSITY OF CHICAGO PRESS

CHICAGO & LONDON

THE UNIVERSITY OF CHICAGO PRESS, CHICAGO 60637
THE UNIVERSITY OF CHICAGO PRESS, LTD., LONDON

International Standard Book Number: 0–226–30774–3
Library of Congress Catalog Card Number: 60–950

NOTE

For this selection from *The Complete Greek Tragedies*, the University of Chicago Press has asked me to write the introductions. Longer and fuller introductions, mostly by the translators themselves, will be found in *The Complete Greek Tragedies*. As befits a limited volume, I have tried to state, very briefly, the essential features of each tragedy here reprinted. The personal views given are, of course, my own, and the translators, other than myself, are not to be held responsible.

R. L.

CONTENTS

AGAMEMNON

Translated by Richmond Lattimore

INTRODUCTION

Agamemnon is the first part of the trilogy known as *The Oresteia*, the other two parts being *The Libation Bearers* and *The Eumenides*. The trilogy was presented in 458 B.C. and won first prize.

According to the legend, in the version used by Aeschylus, Atreus tricked his brother, Thyestes, into devouring his own children, all but one. Thyestes cursed the entire house. In the next generation, Agamemnon and Menelaus, sons of Atreus, were kings in Argos. Helen, wife of Menelaus, fled to Troy with Paris (Alexander). Agamemnon led the expedition to Troy and, to insure its success, sacrificed his daughter, Iphigeneia, to Artemis. Clytaemestra took as her lover Aegisthus, the only surviving son of Thyestes. Agamemnon and Clytaemestra arranged a series of beacons between Argos and Troy, by which he would signal the capture of the city.

It is at this point that *Agamemnon* begins. The action contained in the play itself consists of a short, simple series of events: the return of Agamemnon, his formal reception and entrance into the palace, the murder of Agamemnon and Cassandra, and, at the end, the defiance of Argos and its citizens by Clytaemestra and Aegisthus. The power of the drama lies partly in the dramatic arrangements of these events, but also in the choral lyrics and long speeches, in which the tragic scenes of the past, flashbacks in memory, are made to enlarge and illuminate the action and persons before us: the departure for Troy, the portents, and the sacrifice of Iphigeneia; the relay of beacons to announce the fall of Troy; the fall of the city; the flight of Helen; the wreck of the fleet returning from Troy; and the murder of the children of Thyestes.

NOTE

The translation of *Agamemnon* that is here used first appeared in *Greek Plays in Modern Translation*, edited with an Introduction by Dudley Fitts (New York: Dial Press, 1947). It is used here by kind permission of The Dial Press, Inc. Some alterations have been made, chiefly in the matter of spelling Greek names. Two sections of *Agamemnon*, "The God of War, Money Changer of Dead Bodies," and "The Achaeans Have Got Troy, upon This Very Day," first published in *War and the Poet: A Comprehensive Anthology of the World's Great War Poetry*, edited by Richard Eberhart and Selden Rodman, are used by permission of The Devin-Adair Company.

The translation of this play is based on H. W. Smyth's "Loeb Classical Library" text (London and New York: William Heinemann, Ltd., and G. P. Putnam's Sons, 1926). A few deviations from this text occur where the translator has followed the manuscript readings instead of emendations accepted by Smyth.

Various editions of Greek drama divide the lines of lyric passages in various ways, but editors regularly follow the traditional line numbers whether their own line divisions tally with these numbers or not. This accounts for what may appear to be erratic line numbering in this translation. The line numbering in this translation is that of Smyth's text.

CHARACTERS

Watchman

Clytaemestra

Herald

Agamemnon

Cassandra

Aegisthus

Chorus of Argive Elders

*Attendants of Clytaemestra: of Agamemnon: bodyguard
of Aegisthus (all silent parts)*

Time, directly after the fall of Troy.

AGAMEMNON

SCENE: *Argos, before the palace of King Agamemnon. The Watchman,
who speaks the opening lines, is posted on the roof of the palace.
Clytaemestra's entrances are made from a door in the center of the
stage; all others, from the wings.*

(The Watchman, alone.)

I ask the gods some respite from the weariness
of this watchtime measured by years I lie awake
elbowed upon the Atreidae's roof dogwise to mark
the grand processionals of all the stars of night
burdened with winter and again with heat for men,   5
dynasties in their shining blazoned on the air,
these stars, upon their wane and when the rest arise.

I wait; to read the meaning in that beacon light,
a blaze of fire to carry out of Troy the rumor
and outcry of its capture; to such end a lady's   10
male strength of heart in its high confidence ordains.
Now as this bed stricken with night and drenched with dew
I keep, nor ever with kind dreams for company:
since fear in sleep's place stands forever at my head
against strong closure of my eyes, or any rest: 15
I mince such medicine against sleep failed: I sing,
only to weep again the pity of this house
no longer, as once, administered in the grand way.
Now let there be again redemption from distress,
the flare burning from the blackness in good augury.   20

(A light shows in the distance.)

Oh hail, blaze of the darkness, harbinger of day's
shining, and of processionals and dance and choirs
of multitudes in Argos for this day of grace.
Ahoy!
I cry the news aloud to Agamemnon's queen,   25

that she may rise up from her bed of state with speed
to raise the rumor of gladness welcoming this beacon,
and singing rise, if truly the citadel of Ilium
has fallen, as the shining of this flare proclaims.
I also, I, will make my choral prelude, since   30
my lord's dice cast aright are counted as my own,
and mine the tripled sixes of this torchlit throw.

May it only happen. May my king come home, and I
take up within this hand the hand I love. The rest
I leave to silence; for an ox stands huge upon   35
my tongue. The house itself, could it take voice, might speak
aloud and plain. I speak to those who understand,
but if they fail, I have forgotten everything.

                        (Exit. The Chorus enters, speaking.)

Ten years since the great contestants   40
of Priam's right,
Menelaus and Agamemnon, my lord,
twin throned, twin sceptered, in twofold power
of kings from God, the Atreidae,
put forth from this shore   45
the thousand ships of the Argives,
the strength and the armies.
Their cry of war went shrill from the heart,
as eagles stricken in agony
for young perished, high from the nest   50
eddy and circle
to bend and sweep of the wings' stroke,
lost far below
the fledgelings, the nest, and the tendance.
Yet someone hears in the air, a god,   55
Apollo, Pan, or Zeus, the high
thin wail of these sky-guests, and drives
late to its mark
the Fury upon the transgressors.

So drives Zeus the great guest god   60

the Atreidae against Alexander:
for one woman's promiscuous sake
the struggling masses, legs tired,
knees grinding in dust,
spears broken in the onset.   65
Danaans and Trojans
they have it alike. It goes as it goes
now. The end will be destiny.
You cannot burn flesh or pour unguents,
not innocent cool tears,   70
that will soften the gods' stiff anger.

But we; dishonored, old in our bones,
cast off even then from the gathering horde,
stay here, to prop up
on staves the strength of a baby.   75
Since the young vigor that urges
inward to the heart
is frail as age, no warcraft yet perfect,
while beyond age, leaf
withered, man goes three footed   80
no stronger than a child is,
a dream that falters in daylight.

(Clytaemestra enters quietly. The Chorus continues to speak.)

But you, lady,
daughter of Tyndareus, Clytaemestra, our queen:
What is there to be done? What new thing have you heard? 85
In persuasion of what
report do you order such sacrifice?
To all the gods of the city,
the high and the deep spirits,
to them of the sky and the market places,   90
the altars blaze with oblations.
The staggered flame goes sky high
one place, then another,
drugged by the simple soft

persuasion of sacred unguents,   95
the deep stored oil of the kings.
Of these things what can be told
openly, speak.
Be healer to this perplexity
that grows now into darkness of thought,   100
while again sweet hope shining from the flames
beats back the pitiless pondering
of sorrow that eats my heart.

I have mastery yet to chant the wonder at the wayside
given to kings. Still by God's grace there surges within me   105
singing magic
grown to my life and power,
how the wild bird portent
hurled forth the Achaeans'
twin-stemmed power single hearted,   110
lords of the youth of Hellas,
with spear and hand of strength
to the land of Teucrus.
Kings of birds to the kings of the ships,
one black, one blazed with silver,   115
clear seen by the royal house
on the right, the spear hand,
they lighted, watched by all
tore a hare, ripe, bursting with young unborn yet,
stayed from her last fleet running.   120
Sing sorrow, sorrow: but good win out in the end.

Then the grave seer of the host saw through to the hearts divided,
knew the fighting sons of Atreus feeding on the hare
with the host, their people.
Seeing beyond, he spoke: 125
"With time, this foray
shall stalk the castle of Priam.
Before then, under
the walls, Fate shall spoil

in violence the rich herds of the people.   130
Only let no doom of the gods darken
upon this huge iron forged to curb Troy—
from inward. Artemis the undefiled
is angered with pity
at the flying hounds of her father   135
eating the unborn young in the hare and the shivering mother.
She is sick at the eagles' feasting.
Sing sorrow, sorrow: but good win out in the end.

Lovely you are and kind   140
to the tender young of ravening lions.
For sucklings of all the savage
beasts that lurk in the lonely places you have sympathy.
Grant meaning to these appearances
good, yet not without evil.   145
Healer Apollo, I pray you
let her not with cross winds
bind the ships of the Danaans
to time-long anchorage   150
forcing a second sacrifice unholy, untasted,
working bitterness in the blood
and faith lost. For the terror returns like sickness to lurk in the
      house;
the secret anger remembers the child that shall be avenged."   155
Such, with great good things beside, rang out in the voice of
      Calchas,
these fatal signs from the birds by the way to the house of the
      princes,
wherewith in sympathy
sing sorrow, sorrow: but good win out in the end.

Zeus: whatever he may be, if this name   160
pleases him in invocation,
thus I call upon him.
I have pondered everything
yet I cannot find a way,

only Zeus, to cast this dead weight of ignorance   165
finally from out my brain.

He who in time long ago was great,
throbbing with gigantic strength,
shall be as if he never were, unspoken.   170
He who followed him has found
his master, and is gone.
Cry aloud without fear the victory of Zeus,
you will not have failed the truth: 175

Zeus, who guided men to think,
who has laid it down that wisdom
comes alone through suffering.
Still there drips in sleep against the heart
grief of memory; against   180
our pleasure we are temperate.
From the gods who sit in grandeur
grace comes somehow violent.

On that day the elder king
of the Achaean ships, no more
strict against the prophet's word,   185
turned with the crosswinds of fortune,
when no ship sailed, no pail was full,
and the Achaean people sulked
fast against the shore at Aulis
facing Chalcis, where the tides ebb and surge: 190

and winds blew from the Strymon, bearing
sick idleness, ships tied fast, and hunger,
distraction of the mind, carelessness
for hull and cable;   195
with time's length bent to double measure
by delay crumbled the flower and pride
of Argos. Then against the bitter wind
the seer's voice clashed out
another medicine   200

more hateful yet, and spoke of Artemis, so that the kings
dashed their staves to the ground and could not hold their tears.

The elder lord spoke aloud before them: 205
"My fate is angry if I disobey these,
but angry if I slaughter
this child, the beauty of my house,
with maiden blood shed staining
these father's hands beside the altar.   210
What of these things goes now without disaster?
How shall I fail my ships
and lose my faith of battle?
For them to urge such sacrifice of innocent blood   215
angrily, for their wrath is great—it is right. May all be well yet."

But when necessity's yoke was put upon him
he changed, and from the heart the breath came bitter
and sacrilegious, utterly infidel,   220
to warp a will now to be stopped at nothing.
The sickening in men's minds, tough,
reckless in fresh cruelty brings daring. He endured then
to sacrifice his daughter
to stay the strength of war waged for a woman,   225
first offering for the ships' sake.

Her supplications and her cries of father
were nothing, nor the child's lamentation
to kings passioned for battle.   230
The father prayed, called to his men to lift her
with strength of hand swept in her robes aloft
and prone above the altar, as you might lift
a goat for sacrifice, with guards
against the lips' sweet edge, to check   235
the curse cried on the house of Atreus
by force of bit and speech drowned in strength.

Pouring then to the ground her saffron mantle
she struck the sacrificers with   240
the eyes' arrows of pity,

lovely as in a painted scene, and striving
to speak—as many times
at the kind festive table of her father
she had sung, and in the clear voice of a stainless maiden   245
with love had graced the song
of worship when the third cup was poured.

What happened next I saw not, neither speak it.
The crafts of Calchas fail not of outcome.
Justice so moves that those only learn   250
who suffer; and the future
you shall know when it has come; before then, forget it.
It is grief too soon given.
All will come clear in the next dawn's sunlight.
Let good fortune follow these things as   255
she who is here desires,
our Apian land's singlehearted protectress.

(The Chorus now turns toward Clytaemestra, and the leader
speaks to her.)

I have come in reverence, Clytaemestra, of your power.
For when the man is gone and the throne void, his right
falls to the prince's lady, and honor must be given.   260
Is it some grace—or otherwise—that you have heard
to make you sacrifice at messages of good hope?
I should be glad to hear, but must not blame your silence.

Clytaemestra

As it was said of old, may the dawn child be born
to be an angel of blessing from the kindly night.   265
You shall know joy beyond all you ever hoped to hear.
The men of Argos have taken Priam's citadel.

Chorus

What have you said? Your words escaped my unbelief.

Clytaemestra

The Achaeans are in Troy. Is that not clear enough?

Chorus

This slow delight steals over me to bring forth tears.   270

Clytaemestra

Yes, for your eyes betray the loyal heart within.

Chorus

Yet how can I be certain? Is there some evidence?

Clytaemestra

There is, there must be; unless a god has lied to me.

Chorus

Is it dream visions, easy to believe, you credit?

Clytaemestra

I accept nothing from a brain that is dull with sleep.   275

Chorus

The charm, then, of some rumor, that made rich your hope?

Clytaemestra

Am I some young girl, that you find my thoughts so silly?

Chorus

How long, then, is it since the citadel was stormed?

Clytaemestra

It is the night, the mother of this dawn I hailed.

Chorus

What kind of messenger could come in speed like this?   280

Clytaemestra

Hephaestus, who cast forth the shining blaze from Ida.
And beacon after beacon picking up the flare
carried it here; Ida to the Hermaean horn
of Lemnos, where it shone above the isle, and next
the sheer rock face of Zeus on Athos caught it up;   285
and plunging skyward to arch the shoulders of the sea
the strength of the running flare in exultation,
pine timbers flaming into gold, like the sunrise,

brought the bright message to Macistus' sentinel cliffs,
who, never slow nor in the carelessness of sleep   290
caught up, sent on his relay in the courier chain,
and far across Euripus' streams the beacon flare
carried to signal watchmen on Messapion.
These took it again in turn, and heaping high a pile
of silvery brush flamed it to throw the message on.   295
And the flare sickened never, but grown stronger yet
outleapt the river valley of Asopus like
the very moon for shining, to Cithaeron's scaur
to waken the next station of the flaming post.
These watchers, not contemptuous of the far-thrown blaze,   300
kindled another beacon vaster than commanded.
The light leaned high above Gorgopis' staring marsh,
and striking Aegyplanctus' mountain top, drove on
yet one more relay, lest the flare die down in speed.
Kindled once more with stintless heaping force, they send   305
the beard of flame to hugeness, passing far beyond
the promontory that gazes on the Saronic strait
and flaming far, until it plunged at last to strike
the steep rock of Arachnus near at hand, our watchtower.
And thence there fell upon this house of Atreus' sons   310
the flare whose fathers mount to the Idaean beacon.
These are the changes on my torchlight messengers,
one from another running out the laps assigned.
The first and the last sprinters have the victory.
By such proof and such symbol I announce to you   315
my lord at Troy has sent his messengers to me.

Chorus

The gods, lady, shall have my prayers and thanks straightway.
And yet to hear your story till all wonder fades
would be my wish, could you but tell it once again.

Clytaemestra

The Achaeans have got Troy, upon this very day.   320
I think the city echoes with a clash of cries.

Pour vinegar and oil into the selfsame bowl,
you could not say they mix in friendship, but fight on.
Thus variant sound the voices of the conquerors
and conquered, from the opposition of their fates.   325
Trojans are stooping now to gather in their arms
their dead, husbands and brothers; children lean to clasp
the aged who begot them, crying upon the death
of those most dear, from lips that never will be free.
The Achaeans have their midnight work after the fighting   330
that sets them down to feed on all the city has,
ravenous, headlong, by no rank and file assigned,
but as each man has drawn his shaken lot by chance.
And in the Trojan houses that their spears have taken
they settle now, free of the open sky, the frosts   335
and dampness of the evening; without sentinels set
they sleep the sleep of happiness the whole night through.
And if they reverence the gods who hold the city
and all the holy temples of the captured land,
they, the despoilers, might not be despoiled in turn.   340
Let not their passion overwhelm them; let no lust
seize on these men to violate what they must not.
The run to safety and home is yet to make; they must turn
the pole, and run the backstretch of the double course.
Yet, though the host come home without offence to high   345
gods, even so the anger of these slaughtered men
may never sleep. Oh, let there be no fresh wrong done!

Such are the thoughts you hear from me, a woman merely.
Yet may the best win through, that none may fail to see.
Of all good things to wish this is my dearest choice.   350

Chorus

My lady, no grave man could speak with better grace.
I have listened to the proofs of your tale, and I believe,
and go to make my glad thanksgivings to the gods.
This pleasure is not unworthy of the grief that gave it.

O Zeus our lord and Night beloved,   355
bestower of power and beauty,
you slung above the bastions of Troy
the binding net, that none, neither great
nor young, might outleap
the gigantic toils   360
of enslavement and final disaster.
I gaze in awe on Zeus of the guests
who wrung from Alexander such payment.
He bent the bow with slow care, that neither
the shaft might hurdle the stars, nor fall   365
spent to the earth, short driven.

They have the stroke of Zeus to tell of.
This thing is clear and you may trace it.
He acted as he had decreed. A man thought
the gods deigned not to punish mortals   370
who trampled down the delicacy of things
inviolable. That man was wicked.
The curse on great daring
shines clear; it wrings atonement   375
from those high hearts that drive to evil,
from houses blossoming to pride
and peril. Let there be
wealth without tears; enough for
the wise man who will ask no further.   380
There is not any armor
in gold against perdition
for him who spurns the high altar
of Justice down to the darkness.

Persuasion the persistent overwhelms him,   385
she, strong daughter of designing Ruin.
And every medicine is vain; the sin
smolders not, but burns to evil beauty.
As cheap bronze tortured   390
at the touchstone relapses

to blackness and grime, so this man
tested shows vain
as a child that strives to catch the bird flying
and wins shame that shall bring down his city.   395
No god will hear such a man's entreaty,
but whoso turns to these ways
they strike him down in his wickedness.
This was Paris: he came
to the house of the sons of Atreus,   400
stole the woman away, and shamed
the guest's right of the board shared.

She left among her people the stir and clamor
of shields and of spearheads,   405
the ships to sail and the armor.
She took to Ilium her dowry, death.
She stepped forth lightly between the gates
daring beyond all daring. And the prophets
about the great house wept aloud and spoke:
"Alas, alas for the house and for the champions,   410
alas for the bed signed with their love together.
Here now is silence, scorned, unreproachful.
The agony of his loss is clear before us.
Longing for her who lies beyond the sea
he shall see a phantom queen in his household.   415
Her images in their beauty
are bitterness to her lord now
where in the emptiness of eyes
all passion has faded."

Shining in dreams the sorrowful   420
memories pass; they bring him
vain delight only.
It is vain, to dream and to see splendors,
and the image slipping from the arms' embrace
escapes, not to return again,   425
on wings drifting down the ways of sleep.

Such have the sorrows been in the house by the hearthside;
such have there been, and yet there are worse than these.
In all Hellas, for those who swarmed to the host
the heartbreaking misery   430
shows in the house of each.
Many are they who are touched at the heart by these things.
Those they sent forth they knew;
now, in place of the young men
urns and ashes are carried home   435
to the houses of the fighters.

The god of war, money changer of dead bodies,
held the balance of his spear in the fighting,
and from the corpse-fires at Ilium   440
sent to their dearest the dust
heavy and bitter with tears shed
packing smooth the urns with
ashes that once were men.
They praise them through their tears, how this man   445
knew well the craft of battle, how another
went down splendid in the slaughter:
and all for some strange woman.
Thus they mutter in secrecy,
and the slow anger creeps below their grief   450
at Atreus' sons and their quarrels.
There by the walls of Ilium
the young men in their beauty keep
graves deep in the alien soil
they hated and they conquered.   455

The citizens speak: their voice is dull with hatred.
The curse of the people must be paid for.
There lurks for me in the hooded night
terror of what may be told me.   460
The gods fail not to mark
those who have killed many.
The black Furies stalking the man

fortunate beyond all right
wrench back again the set of his life   465
and drop him to darkness. There among
the ciphers there is no more comfort
in power. And the vaunt of high glory
is bitterness; for God's thunderbolts
crash on the towering mountains.   470
Let me attain no envied wealth,
let me not plunder cities,
neither be taken in turn, and face
life in the power of another.

(*Various members of the Chorus, speaking severally.*)

From the beacon's bright message   475
the fleet rumor runs
through the city. If this be real
who knows? Perhaps the gods have sent some lie to us.

Who of us is so childish or so reft of wit
that by the beacon's messages   480
his heart flamed must despond again
when the tale changes in the end?

It is like a woman indeed
to take the rapture before the fact has shown for true.

They believe too easily, are too quick to shift   485
from ground to ground; and swift indeed
the rumor voiced by a woman dies again.

Now we shall understand these torches and their shining,
the beacons, and the interchange of flame and flame.   490
They may be real; yet bright and dreamwise ecstasy
in light's appearance might have charmed our hearts awry.
I see a herald coming from the beach, his brows
shaded with sprigs of olive; and upon his feet
the dust, dry sister of the mire, makes plain to me   495
that he will find a voice, not merely kindle flame
from mountain timber, and make signals from the smoke,

but tell us outright, whether to be happy, or—
but I shrink back from naming the alternative.
That which appeared was good; may yet more good be given.   500

And any man who prays that different things befall
the city, may he reap the crime of his own heart.

(The Herald enters, and speaks.)

Soil of my fathers, Argive earth I tread upon,
in daylight of the tenth year I have come back to you.
All my hopes broke but one, and this I have at last.   505
I never could have dared to dream that I might die
in Argos, and be buried in this beloved soil.
Hail to the Argive land and to its sunlight, hail
to its high sovereign, Zeus, and to the Pythian king.
May you no longer shower your arrows on our heads.   510
Beside Scamandrus you were grim; be satisfied
and turn to savior now and healer of our hurts,
my lord Apollo. Gods of the market place assembled,
I greet you all, and my own patron deity
Hermes, beloved herald, in whose right all heralds   515
are sacred; and you heroes that sent forth the host,
propitiously take back all that the spear has left.
O great hall of the kings and house beloved; seats
of sanctity; divinities that face the sun:
if ever before, look now with kind and glowing eyes   520
to greet our king in state after so long a time.
He comes, lord Agamemnon, bearing light in gloom
to you, and to all that are assembled here.
Salute him with good favor, as he well deserves,
the man who has wrecked Ilium with the spade of Zeus   525
vindictive, whereby all their plain has been laid waste.
Gone are their altars, the sacred places of the gods
are gone, and scattered all the seed within the ground.
With such a yoke as this gripped to the neck of Troy
he comes, the king, Atreus' elder son, a man   530

fortunate to be honored far above all men
alive; not Paris nor the city tied to him
can boast he did more than was done him in return.
Guilty of rape and theft, condemned, he lost the prize
captured, and broke to sheer destruction all the house   535
of his fathers, with the very ground whereon it stood.
Twice over the sons of Priam have atoned their sins.

Chorus
Hail and be glad, herald of the Achaean host.

Herald
I am happy; I no longer ask the gods for death.

Chorus
Did passion for your country so strip bare your heart?   540

Herald
So that the tears broke in my eyes, for happiness.

Chorus
You were taken with that sickness, then, that brings delight.

Herald
How? I cannot deal with such words until I understand.

Chorus
Struck with desire of those who loved as much again.

Herald
You mean our country longed for us, as we for home?   545

Chorus
So that I sighed, out of the darkness of my heart.

Herald
Whence came this black thought to afflict the mind with fear?

Chorus
Long since it was my silence kept disaster off.

Herald
But how? There were some you feared when the kings went
away?

Chorus
So much that as you said now, even death were grace.   550

Herald

Well: the end has been good. And in the length of time
part of our fortune you could say held favorable,
but part we cursed again. And who, except the gods,
can live time through forever without any pain?
Were I to tell you of the hard work done, the nights   555
exposed, the cramped sea-quarters, the foul beds—what part
of day's disposal did we not cry out loud?
Ashore, the horror stayed with us and grew. We lay
against the ramparts of our enemies, and from
the sky, and from the ground, the meadow dews came out   560
to soak our clothes and fill our hair with lice. And if
I were to tell of winter time, when all birds died,
the snows of Ida past endurance she sent down,
or summer heat, when in the lazy noon the sea
fell level and asleep under a windless sky—   565
but why live such grief over again? That time is gone
for us, and gone for those who died. Never again
need they rise up, nor care again for anything.
Why must a live man count the numbers of the slain,
why grieve at fortune's wrath that fades to break once more?   570
I call a long farewell to all our unhappiness.
For us, survivors of the Argive armament,
the pleasure wins, pain casts no weight in the opposite scale.
And here, in this sun's shining, we can boast aloud,
whose fame has gone with wings across the land and sea: 575
"Upon a time the Argive host took Troy, and on
the houses of the gods who live in Hellas nailed
the spoils, to be the glory of days long ago."
And they who hear such things shall call this city blest
and the leaders of the host; and high the grace of God   580
shall be exalted, that did this. You have the story.

Chorus

I must give way; your story shows that I was wrong.
Old men are always young enough to learn, with profit.

But Clytaemestra and her house must hear, above
others, this news that makes luxurious my life.   585

(Clytaemestra comes forward and speaks.)

I raised my cry of joy, and it was long ago
when the first beacon flare of message came by night
to speak of capture and of Ilium's overthrow.
But there was one who laughed at me, who said: "You trust   590
in beacons so, and you believe that Troy has fallen?
How like a woman, for the heart to lift so light."
Men spoke like that; they thought I wandered in my wits;
yet I made sacrifice, and in the womanish strain
voice after voice caught up the cry along the city   595
to echo in the temples of the gods and bless
and still the fragrant flame that melts the sacrifice.

Why should you tell me then the whole long tale at large
when from my lord himself I shall hear all the story?
But now, how best to speed my preparation to   600
receive my honored lord come home again—what else
is light more sweet for woman to behold than this,
to spread the gates before her husband home from war
and saved by God's hand?—take this message to the king.
Come, and with speed, back to the city that longs for him,   605
and may he find a wife within his house as true
as on the day he left her, watchdog of the house
gentle to him alone, fierce to his enemies,
and such a woman in all her ways as this, who has
not broken the seal upon her in the length of days.   610
With no man else have I known delight, nor any shame
of evil speech, more than I know how to temper bronze.

(Clytaemestra goes to the back of the stage.)

Herald

A vaunt like this, so loaded as it is with truth,
it well becomes a highborn lady to proclaim.

Chorus

> Thus has she spoken to you, and well you understand,   615
> words that impress interpreters whose thought is clear.
> But tell me, herald; I would learn of Menelaus,
> that power beloved in this land. Has he survived
> also, and come with you back to his home again?

Herald

> I know no way to lie and make my tale so fair   620
> that friends could reap joy of it for any length of time.

Chorus

> Is there no means to speak us fair, and yet tell the truth?
> It will not hide, when truth and good are torn asunder.

Herald

> He is gone out of the sight of the Achaean host,
> vessel and man alike. I speak no falsehood there.   625

Chorus

> Was it when he had put out from Ilium in your sight,
> or did a storm that struck you both whirl him away?

Herald

> How like a master bowman you have hit the mark
> and in your speech cut a long sorrow to brief stature.

Chorus

> But then the rumor in the host that sailed beside,   630
> was it that he had perished, or might yet be living?

Herald

> No man knows. There is none could tell us that for sure
> except the Sun, from whom this earth has life and increase.

Chorus

> How did this storm, by wrath of the divinities,
> strike on our multitude at sea? How did it end?   635

Herald

> It is not well to stain the blessing of this day
> with speech of evil weight. Such gods are honored apart.

And when the messenger of a shaken host, sad faced,
brings to his city news it prayed never to hear,
this scores one wound upon the body of the people;   640
and that from many houses many men are slain
by the two-lashed whip dear to the War God's hand, this turns
disaster double-bladed, bloodily made two.
The messenger so freighted with a charge of tears
should make his song of triumph at the Furies' door.   645
But, carrying the fair message of our hopes' salvation,
come home to a glad city's hospitality,
how shall I mix my gracious news with foul, and tell
of the storm on the Achaeans by God's anger sent?
For they, of old the deepest enemies, sea and fire,   650
made a conspiracy and gave the oath of hand
to blast in ruin our unhappy Argive army.
At night the sea began to rise in waves of death.
Ship against ship the Thracian stormwind shattered us,
and gored and split, our vessels, swept in violence   655
of storm and whirlwind, beaten by the breaking rain,
drove on in darkness, spun by the wicked shepherd's hand.
But when the sun came up again to light the dawn,
we saw the Aegaean Sea blossoming with dead men,
the men of Achaea, and the wreckage of their ships.   660
For us, and for our ship, some god, no man, by guile
or by entreaty's force prevailing, laid his hand
upon the helm and brought us through with hull unscarred.
Life-giving fortune deigned to take our ship in charge
that neither riding in deep water she took the surf   665
nor drove to shoal and break upon some rocky shore.
But then, delivered from death at sea, in the pale day,
incredulous of our own luck, we shepherded
in our sad thoughts the fresh disaster of the fleet
so pitifully torn and shaken by the storm.   670
Now of these others, if there are any left alive
they speak of us as men who perished, must they not?
Even as we, who fear that they are gone. But may

it all come well in the end. For Menelaus: be sure
if any of them come back that he will be the first.   675
If he is still where some sun's gleam can track him down,
alive and open-eyed, by blessed hand of God
who willed that not yet should his seed be utterly gone,
there is some hope that he will still come home again.
You have heard all; and be sure, you have heard the truth.   680

(The Herald goes out.)

Chorus

Who is he that named you so
fatally in every way?
Could it be some mind unseen
in divination of your destiny
shaping to the lips that name   685
for the bride of spears and blood,
Helen, which is death? Appropriately
death of ships, death of men and cities
from the bower's soft curtained   690
and secluded luxury she sailed then,
driven on the giant west wind,
and armored men in their thousands came,
huntsmen down the oar blade's fading footprint   695
to struggle in blood with those
who by the banks of Simoeis
beached their hulls where the leaves break.

And on Ilium in truth
in the likeness of the name   700
the sure purpose of the Wrath drove
marriage with death: for the guest board
shamed, and Zeus kindly to strangers,
the vengeance wrought on those men
who graced in too loud voice the bride-song   705
fallen to their lot to sing,
the kinsmen and the brothers.
And changing its song's measure

the ancient city of Priam   710
chants in high strain of lamentation,
calling Paris him of the fatal marriage;
for it endured its life's end
in desolation and tears
and the piteous blood of its people.   715

Once a man fostered in his house
a lion cub, from the mother's milk
torn, craving the breast given.
In the first steps of its young life   720
mild, it played with children
and delighted the old.
Caught in the arm's cradle
they pampered it like a newborn child,
shining eyed and broken to the hand   725
to stay the stress of its hunger.

But it grew with time, and the lion
in the blood strain came out; it paid
grace to those who had fostered it
in blood and death for the sheep flocks,   730
a grim feast forbidden.
The house reeked with blood run
nor could its people beat down the bane,
the giant murderer's onslaught.
This thing they raised in their house was blessed   735
by God to be priest of destruction.

And that which first came to the city of Ilium,
call it a dream of calm
and the wind dying,
the loveliness and luxury of much gold,   740
the melting shafts of the eyes' glances,
the blossom that breaks the heart with longing.
But she turned in mid-step of her course to make
bitter the consummation,   745

whirling on Priam's people
to blight with her touch and nearness.
Zeus hospitable sent her,
a vengeance to make brides weep.

It has been made long since and grown old among men,   750
this saying: human wealth
grown to fulness of stature
breeds again nor dies without issue.
From high good fortune in the blood   755
blossoms the quenchless agony.
Far from others I hold my own
mind; only the act of evil
breeds others to follow,
young sins in its own likeness.   760
Houses clear in their right are given
children in all loveliness.

But Pride aging is made
in men's dark actions
ripe with the young pride   765
late or soon when the dawn of destiny
comes and birth is given
to the spirit none may fight nor beat down,
sinful Daring; and in those halls
the black visaged Disasters stamped   770
in the likeness of their fathers.

And Righteousness is a shining in
the smoke of mean houses.
Her blessing is on the just man.   775
From high halls starred with gold by reeking hands
she turns back
with eyes that glance away to the simple in heart,
spurning the strength of gold
stamped false with flattery.   780
And all things she steers to fulfilment.

(Agamemnon enters in a chariot, with Cassandra beside
him. The Chorus speaks to him.)

Behold, my king: sacker of Troy's citadel,
own issue of Atreus.
How shall I hail you? How give honor   785
not crossing too high nor yet bending short
of this time's graces?
For many among men are they who set high
the show of honor, yet break justice.
If one be unhappy, all else are fain   790
to grieve with him: yet the teeth of sorrow
come nowise near to the heart's edge.
And in joy likewise they show joy's semblance,
and torture the face to the false smile.
Yet the good shepherd, who knows his flock,   795
the eyes of men cannot lie to him,
that with water of feigned
love seem to smile from the true heart.
But I: when you marshalled this armament
for Helen's sake, I will not hide it,   800
in ugly style you were written in my heart
for steering aslant the mind's course
to bring home by blood
sacrifice and dead men that wild spirit.
But now, in love drawn up from the deep heart,   805
not skimmed at the edge, we hail you.
You have won, your labor is made gladness.
Ask all men: you will learn in time
which of your citizens have been just
in the city's sway, which were reckless.   810

Agamemnon

To Argos first, and to the gods within the land,
I must give due greeting; they have worked with me to bring
me home; they helped me in the vengeance I have wrought
on Priam's city. Not from the lips of men the gods
heard justice, but in one firm cast they laid their votes   815

within the urn of blood that Ilium must die
and all her people; while above the opposite vase
the hand hovered and there was hope, but no vote fell.
The stormclouds of their ruin live; the ash that dies
upon them gushes still in smoke their pride of wealth.   820
For all this we must thank the gods with grace of much
high praise and memory, we who fenced within our toils
of wrath the city; and, because one woman strayed,
the beast of Argos broke them, the fierce young within
the horse, the armored people who marked out their leap   825
against the setting of the Pleiades. A wild
and bloody lion swarmed above the towers of Troy
to glut its hunger lapping at the blood of kings.

This to the gods, a prelude strung to length of words.
But, for the thought you spoke, I heard and I remember   830
and stand behind you. For I say that it is true.
In few men is it part of nature to respect
a friend's prosperity without begrudging him,
as envy's wicked poison settling to the heart
piles up the pain in one sick with unhappiness,   835
who, staggered under sufferings that are all his own,
winces again to the vision of a neighbor's bliss.
And I can speak, for I have seen, I know it well,
this mirror of companionship, this shadow's ghost,
these men who seemed my friends in all sincerity.   840
One man of them all, Odysseus, he who sailed unwilling,
once yoked to me carried his harness, nor went slack.
Dead though he be or living, I can say it still.

Now in the business of the city and the gods
we must ordain full conclave of all citizens   845
and take our counsel. We shall see what element
is strong, and plan that it shall keep its virtue still.
But that which must be healed—we must use medicine,
or burn, or amputate, with kind intention, take
all means at hand that might beat down corruption's pain. 850

So to the King's house and the home about the hearth
I take my way, with greeting to the gods within
who sent me forth, and who have brought me home once more.
My prize was conquest; may it never fail again.

(Clytaemestra comes forward and speaks.)

Grave gentlemen of Argolis assembled here,   855
I take no shame to speak aloud before you all
the love I bear my husband. In the lapse of time
modesty fades; it is human.

      What I tell you now
I learned not from another; this is my own sad life
all the long years this man was gone at Ilium.   860
It is evil and a thing of terror when a wife
sits in the house forlorn with no man by, and hears
rumors that like a fever die to break again,
and men come in with news of fear, and on their heels
another messenger, with worse news to cry aloud   865
here in this house. Had Agamemnon taken all
the wounds the tale whereof was carried home to me,
he had been cut full of gashes like a fishing net.
If he had died each time that rumor told his death,
he must have been some triple-bodied Geryon   870
back from the dead with threefold cloak of earth upon
his body, and killed once for every shape assumed.
Because such tales broke out forever on my rest,
many a time they cut me down and freed my throat   875
from the noose overslung where I had caught it fast.
And therefore is your son, in whom my love and yours
are sealed and pledged, not here to stand with us today,
Orestes. It were right; yet do not be amazed.
Strophius of Phocis, comrade in arms and faithful friend   880
to you, is keeping him. He spoke to me of peril
on two counts; of your danger under Ilium,
and here, of revolution and the clamorous people
who might cast down the council—since it lies in men's

nature to trample on the fighter already down.   885
Such my excuse to you, and without subterfuge.

For me: the rippling springs that were my tears have dried
utterly up, nor left one drop within. I keep
the pain upon my eyes where late at night I wept
over the beacons long ago set for your sake,   890
untended left forever. In the midst of dreams
the whisper that a gnat's thin wings could winnow broke
my sleep apart. I thought I saw you suffer wounds
more than the time that slept with me could ever hold.

Now all my suffering is past, with griefless heart   895
I hail this man, the watchdog of the fold and hall;
the stay that keeps the ship alive; the post to grip
groundward the towering roof; a father's single child;
land seen by sailors after all their hope was gone;
splendor of daybreak shining from the night of storm;   900
the running spring a parched wayfarer strays upon.
Oh, it is sweet to escape from all necessity!

Such is my greeting to him, that he well deserves.
Let none bear malice; for the harm that went before
I took, and it was great.
                        Now, my beloved one,   905
step from your chariot; yet let not your foot, my lord,
sacker of Ilium, touch the earth. My maidens there!
Why this delay? Your task has been appointed you,
to strew the ground before his feet with tapestries.
Let there spring up into the house he never hoped   910
to see, where Justice leads him in, a crimson path.

In all things else, my heart's unsleeping care shall act
with the gods' aid to set aright what fate ordained.

                        (*Clytaemestra's handmaidens spread a bright carpet
                        between the chariot and the door.*)

Agamemnon

Daughter of Leda, you who kept my house for me,
there is one way your welcome matched my absence well.   915

You strained it to great length. Yet properly to praise
me thus belongs by right to other lips, not yours.
And all this—do not try in woman's ways to make
me delicate, nor, as if I were some Asiatic
bow down to earth and with wide mouth cry out to me,   920
nor cross my path with jealousy by strewing the ground
with robes. Such state becomes the gods, and none beside.
I am a mortal, a man; I cannot trample upon
these tinted splendors without fear thrown in my path.
I tell you, as a man, not god, to reverence me.   925
Discordant is the murmur at such treading down
of lovely things; while God's most lordly gift to man
is decency of mind. Call that man only blest
who has in sweet tranquillity brought his life to close.
If I could only act as such, my hope is good.   930

Clytaemestra

Yet tell me this one thing, and do not cross my will.

Agamemnon

My will is mine. I shall not make it soft for you.

Clytaemestra

It was in fear surely that you vowed this course to God.

Agamemnon

No man has spoken knowing better what he said.

Clytaemestra

If Priam had won as you have, what would he have done?   935

Agamemnon

I well believe he might have walked on tapestries.

Clytaemestra

Be not ashamed before the bitterness of men.

Agamemnon

The people murmur, and their voice is great in strength.

Clytaemestra

Yet he who goes unenvied shall not be admired.

Agamemnon

Surely this lust for conflict is not womanlike?   940

Clytaemestra

Yet for the mighty even to give way is grace.

Agamemnon

Does such a victory as this mean so much to you?

Clytaemestra

Oh yield! The power is yours. Give way of your free will.

Agamemnon

Since you must have it—here, let someone with all speed
take off these sandals, slaves for my feet to tread upon.   945
And as I crush these garments stained from the rich sea
let no god's eyes of hatred strike me from afar.
Great the extravagance, and great the shame I feel
to spoil such treasure and such silver's worth of webs.

So much for all this. Take this stranger girl within   950
now, and be kind. The conqueror who uses softly
his power, is watched from far in the kind eyes of God,
and this slave's yoke is one no man will wear from choice.
Gift of the host to me, and flower exquisite
from all my many treasures, she attends me here.   955

Now since my will was bent to listen to you in this
my feet crush purple as I pass within the hall.

Clytaemestra

The sea is there, and who shall drain its yield? It breeds
precious as silver, ever of itself renewed,
the purple ooze wherein our garments shall be dipped.   960
And by God's grace this house keeps full sufficiency
of all. Poverty is a thing beyond its thought.
I could have vowed to trample many splendors down

had such decree been ordained from the oracles
those days when all my study was to bring home your life.   965
For when the root lives yet the leaves will come again
to fence the house with shade against the Dog Star's heat,
and now you have come home to keep your hearth and house
you bring with you the symbol of our winter's warmth;
but when Zeus ripens the green clusters into wine   970
there shall be coolness in the house upon those days
because the master ranges his own halls once more.

Zeus, Zeus accomplisher, accomplish these my prayers.
Let your mind bring these things to pass. It is your will.

(*Agamemnon and Clytaemestra enter the house. Cassandra
remains in the chariot. The Chorus speaks.*)

Why must this persistent fear   975
beat its wings so ceaselessly
and so close against my mantic heart?
Why this strain unwanted, unrepaid, thus prophetic?
Nor can valor of good hope   980
seated near the chambered depth
of the spirit cast it out
as dreams of dark fancy; and yet time
has buried in the mounding sand
the sea cables since that day   985
when against Ilium
the army and the ships put to sea.

Yet I have seen with these eyes
Agamemnon home again.
Still the spirit sings, drawing deep   990
from within this unlyric threnody of the Fury.
Hope is gone utterly,
the sweet strength is far away.
Surely this is not fantasy.   995
Surely it is real, this whirl of drifts
that spin the stricken heart.
Still I pray; may all this

expectation fade as vanity
into unfulfilment, and not be.   1000

Yet it is true: the high strength of men
knows no content with limitation. Sickness
chambered beside it beats at the wall between.
Man's fate that sets a true   1005
course yet may strike upon
the blind and sudden reefs of disaster.
But if before such time, fear
throw overboard some precious thing
of the cargo, with deliberate cast,   1010
not all the house, laboring
with weight of ruin, shall go down,
nor sink the hull deep within the sea.
And great and affluent the gift of Zeus
in yield of ploughed acres year on year   1015
makes void again sick starvation.

But when the black and mortal blood of man
has fallen to the ground before his feet, who then   1020
can sing spells to call it back again?
Did Zeus not warn us once
when he struck to impotence
that one who could in truth charm back the dead men?
Had the gods not so ordained   1025
that fate should stand against fate
to check any man's excess,
my heart now would have outrun speech
to break forth the water of its grief.
But this is so; I murmur deep in darkness   1030
sore at heart; my hope is gone now
ever again to unwind some crucial good
from the flames about my heart.

> (*Clytaemestra comes out from the house again*
> *and speaks to Cassandra.*)

Cassandra, you may go within the house as well,   1035
since Zeus in no unkindness has ordained that you

must share our lustral water, stand with the great throng
of slaves that flock to the altar of our household god.
Step from this chariot, then, and do not be so proud.
And think—they say that long ago Alcmena's son   1040
was sold in bondage and endured the bread of slaves.
But if constraint of fact forces you to such fate,
be glad indeed for masters ancient in their wealth.
They who have reaped success beyond their dreams of hope
are savage above need and standard toward their slaves.   1045
From us you shall have all you have the right to ask.

Chorus

What she has spoken is for you, and clear enough.
Fenced in these fatal nets wherein you find yourself
you should obey her if you can; perhaps you can not.

Clytaemestra

Unless she uses speech incomprehensible,   1050
barbarian, wild as the swallow's song, I speak
within her understanding, and she must obey.

Chorus

Go with her. What she bids is best in circumstance
that rings you now. Obey, and leave this carriage seat.

Clytaemestra

I have no leisure to stand outside the house and waste   1055
time on this woman. At the central altarstone
the flocks are standing, ready for the sacrifice
we make to this glad day we never hoped to see.
You: if you are obeying my commands at all, be quick.
But if in ignorance you fail to comprehend,   1060
speak not, but make with your barbarian hand some sign.

Chorus

I think this stranger girl needs some interpreter
who understands. She is like some captive animal.

Clytaemestra

No, she is in the passion of her own wild thoughts.
Leaving her captured city she has come to us   1065

untrained to take the curb, and will not understand
until her rage and strength have foamed away in blood.
I shall throw down no more commands for her contempt.

(*Clytaemestra goes back into the house.*)

Chorus

I, though, shall not be angry, for I pity her.
Come down, poor creature, leave the empty car. Give way   1070
to compulsion and take up the yoke that shall be yours.

(*Cassandra descends from the chariot and cries out loud.*)

Oh shame upon the earth!
Apollo, Apollo!

Chorus

You cry on Loxias in agony? He is not
of those immortals the unhappy supplicate.   1075

Cassandra

Oh shame upon the earth!
Apollo, Apollo!

Chorus

Now once again in bitter voice she calls upon
this god, who has not part in any lamentation.

Cassandra

Apollo, Apollo!   1080
Lord of the ways, my ruin.
You have undone me once again, and utterly.

Chorus

I think she will be prophetic of her own disaster.
Even in the slave's heart the gift divine lives on.

Cassandra

Apollo, Apollo!   1085
Lord of the ways, my ruin.
Where have you led me now at last? What house is this?

Chorus

> The house of the Atreidae. If you understand
> not that, I can tell you; and so much at least is true.

Cassandra

> No, but a house that God hates, guilty within   1090
> of kindred blood shed, torture of its own,
> the shambles for men's butchery, the dripping floor.

Chorus

> The stranger is keen scented like some hound upon
> the trail of blood that leads her to discovered death.

Cassandra

> Behold there the witnesses to my faith.   1095
> The small children wail for their own death
> and the flesh roasted that their father fed upon.

Chorus

> We had been told before of this prophetic fame
> of yours: we want no prophets in this place at all.

Cassandra

> Ah, for shame, what can she purpose now?   1100
> What is this new and huge
> stroke of atrocity she plans within the house
> to beat down the beloved beyond hope of healing?
> Rescue is far away.

Chorus

> I can make nothing of these prophecies. The rest   1105
> I understood; the city is full of the sound of them.

Cassandra

> So cruel then, that you can do this thing?
> The husband of your own bed
> to bathe bright with water—how shall I speak the end?
> This thing shall be done with speed. The hand gropes now, **and**
>   the other   1110
> hand follows in turn.

Chorus

> No, I am lost. After the darkness of her speech
> I go bewildered in a mist of prophecies.

Cassandra

> No, no, see there! What is that thing that shows?
> Is it some net of death?   1115
> Or is the trap the woman there, the murderess?
> Let now the slakeless fury in the race
> rear up to howl aloud over this monstrous death.

Chorus

> Upon what demon in the house do you call, to raise
> the cry of triumph? All your speech makes dark my hope.   1120
> And to the heart below trickles the pale drop
> as in the hour of death
> timed to our sunset and the mortal radiance.
> Ruin is near, and swift.

Cassandra

> See there, see there! Keep from his mate the bull.   1125
> Caught in the folded web's
> entanglement she pinions him and with the black horn
> strikes. And he crumples in the watered bath.
> Guile, I tell you, and death there in the caldron wrought.

Chorus

> I am not proud in skill to guess at prophecies,   1130
> yet even I can see the evil in this thing.
> From divination what good ever has come to men?
> Art, and multiplication of words
> drifting through tangled evil bring
> terror to them that hear.   1135

Cassandra

> Alas, alas for the wretchedness of my ill-starred life.
> This pain flooding the song of sorrow is mine alone.
> Why have you brought me here in all unhappiness?
> Why, why? Except to die with him? What else could be?

Chorus

> You are possessed of God, mazed at heart   1140
> to sing your own death
> song, the wild lyric as
> in clamor for Itys, Itys over and over again
> her long life of tears weeping forever grieves
> the brown nightingale.   1145

Cassandra

> Oh for the nightingale's pure song and a fate like hers.
> With fashion of beating wings the gods clothed her about
> and a sweet life gave her and without lamentation.
> But mine is the sheer edge of the tearing iron.

Chorus

> Whence come, beat upon beat, driven of God,   1150
> vain passions of tears?
> Whence your cries, terrified, clashing in horror,
> in wrought melody and the singing speech?
> Whence take you the marks to this path of prophecy
> and speech of terror?   1155

Cassandra

> Oh marriage of Paris, death to the men beloved!
> Alas, Scamandrus, water my fathers drank.
> There was a time I too at your springs
> drank and grew strong. Ah me,
> for now beside the deadly rivers, Cocytus   1160
> and Acheron, I must cry out my prophecies.

Chorus

> What is this word, too clear, you have uttered now?
> A child could understand.
> And deep within goes the stroke of the dripping fang
> as mortal pain at the trebled song of your agony   1165
> shivers the heart to hear.

Cassandra

> O sorrow, sorrow of my city dragged to uttermost death.
> O sacrifices my father made at the wall.

Flocks of the pastured sheep slaughtered there.
And no use at all   1170
to save our city from its pain inflicted now.
And I too, with brain ablaze in fever, shall go down.

Chorus

This follows the run of your song.
Is it, in cruel force of weight,
some divinity kneeling upon you brings   1175
the death song of your passionate suffering?
I can not see the end.

Cassandra

No longer shall my prophecies like some young girl
new-married glance from under veils, but bright and strong
as winds blow into morning and the sun's uprise   1180
shall wax along the swell like some great wave, to burst
at last upon the shining of this agony.
Now I will tell you plainly and from no cryptic speech;
bear me then witness, running at my heels upon
the scent of these old brutal things done long ago.   1185
There is a choir that sings as one, that shall not again
leave this house ever; the song thereof breaks harsh with menace.
And drugged to double fury on the wine of men's
blood shed, there lurks forever here a drunken rout
of ingrown vengeful spirits never to be cast forth.   1190
Hanging above the hall they chant their song of hate
and the old sin; and taking up the strain in turn
spit curses on that man who spoiled his brother's bed.
Did I go wide, or hit, like a real archer? Am I
some swindling seer who hawks his lies from door to door?   1195
Upon your oath, bear witness that I know by heart
the legend of ancient wickedness within this house.

Chorus

And how could an oath, though cast in rigid honesty,
do any good? And still we stand amazed at you,

reared in an alien city far beyond the sea,   1200
   how can you strike, as if you had been there, the truth.

Cassandra

   Apollo was the seer who set me to this work.

Chorus

   Struck with some passion for you, and himself a god?

Cassandra

   There was a time I blushed to speak about these things.

Chorus

   True; they who prosper take on airs of vanity.   1205

Cassandra

   Yes, then; he wrestled with me, and he breathed delight.

Chorus

   Did you come to the getting of children then, as people do?

Cassandra

   I promised that to Loxias, but I broke my word.

Chorus

   Were you already ecstatic in the skills of God?

Cassandra

   Yes; even then I read my city's destinies.   1210

Chorus

   So Loxias' wrath did you no harm? How could that be?

Cassandra

   For this my trespass, none believed me ever again.

Chorus

   But we do; all that you foretell seems true to us.

Cassandra

   But this is evil, see!
   Now once again the pain of grim, true prophecy   1215
   shivers my whirling brain in a storm of things foreseen.

Look there, see what is hovering above the house,
so small and young, imaged as in the shadow of dreams,
like children almost, killed by those most dear to them,
and their hands filled with their own flesh, as food to eat. 1220
I see them holding out the inward parts, the vitals,
oh pitiful, that meat their father tasted of. . . .
I tell you: There is one that plots vengeance for this,
the strengthless lion rolling in his master's bed,
who keeps, ah me, the house against his lord's return; 1225
my lord too, now that I wear the slave's yoke on my neck.
King of the ships, who tore up Ilium by the roots,
what does he know of this accursed bitch, who licks
his hand, who fawns on him with lifted ears, who like
a secret death shall strike the coward's stroke, nor fail? 1230
No, this is daring when the female shall strike down
the male. What can I call her and be right? What beast
of loathing? Viper double-fanged, or Scylla witch
holed in the rocks and bane of men that range the sea;
smoldering mother of death to smoke relentless hate 1235
on those most dear. How she stood up and howled aloud
and unashamed, as at the breaking point of battle,
in feigned gladness for his salvation from the sea!
What does it matter now if men believe or no?
What is to come will come. And soon you too will stand 1240
beside, to murmur in pity that my words were true.

Chorus

Thyestes' feast upon the flesh of his own children
I understand in terror at the thought, and fear
is on me hearing truth and no tale fabricated.
The rest: I heard it, but wander still far from the course. 1245

Cassandra

I tell you, you shall look on Agamemnon dead.

Chorus

Peace, peace, poor woman; put those bitter lips to sleep.

Cassandra

Useless; there is no god of healing in this story.

Chorus

Not if it must be; may it somehow fail to come.

Cassandra

Prayers, yes; they do not pray; they plan to strike, and kill.   1250

Chorus

What man is it who moves this beastly thing to be?

Cassandra

What man? You did mistake my divination then.

Chorus

It may be; I could not follow through the schemer's plan.

Cassandra

Yet I know Greek; I think I know it far too well.

Chorus

And Pythian oracles are Greek, yet hard to read.   1255

Cassandra

Oh, flame and pain that sweeps me once again! My lord,
Apollo, King of Light, the pain, aye me, the pain!
This is the woman-lioness, who goes to bed
with the wolf, when her proud lion ranges far away,
and she will cut me down; as a wife mixing drugs   1260
she wills to shred the virtue of my punishment
into her bowl of wrath as she makes sharp the blade
against her man, death that he brought a mistress home.
Why do I wear these mockeries upon my body,
this staff of prophecy, these flowers at my throat?   1265
At least I will spoil you before I die. Out, down,
break, damn you! This for all that you have done to me.
Make someone else, not me, luxurious in disaster. . . .
Lo now, this is Apollo who has stripped me here
of my prophetic robes. He watched me all the time   1270

wearing this glory, mocked of all, my dearest ones
who hated me with all their hearts, so vain, so wrong;
called like some gypsy wandering from door to door
beggar, corrupt, half-starved, and I endured it all.
And now the seer has done with me, his prophetess,   1275
and led me into such a place as this, to die.
Lost are my father's altars, but the block is there
to reek with sacrificial blood, my own. We two
must die, yet die not vengeless by the gods. For there
shall come one to avenge us also, born to slay   1280
his mother, and to wreak death for his father's blood.
Outlaw and wanderer, driven far from his own land,
he will come back to cope these stones of inward hate.
For this is a strong oath and sworn by the high gods,
that he shall cast men headlong for his father felled.   1285
Why am I then so pitiful? Why must I weep?
Since once I saw the citadel of Ilium
die as it died, and those who broke the city, doomed
by the gods, fare as they have fared accordingly,
I will go through with it. I too will take my fate.   1290
I call as on the gates of death upon these gates
to pray only for this thing, that the stroke be true,
and that with no convulsion, with a rush of blood
in painless death, I may close up these eyes, and rest.

Chorus

O woman much enduring and so greatly wise,   1295
you have said much. But if this thing you know be true,
this death that comes upon you, how can you, serene,
walk to the altar like a driven ox of God?

Cassandra

Friends, there is no escape for any longer time.

Chorus

Yet longest left in time is to be honored still.   1300

Cassandra

The day is here and now; I can not win by flight.

Chorus

Woman, be sure your heart is brave; you can take much.

Cassandra

None but the unhappy people ever hear such praise.

Chorus

Yet there is a grace on mortals who so nobly die.

Cassandra

Alas for you, father, and for your lordly sons.   1305
Ah!

Chorus

What now? What terror whirls you backward from the door?

Cassandra

Foul, foul!

Chorus

What foulness then, unless some horror in the mind?

Cassandra

That room within reeks with blood like a slaughter house.

Chorus

What then? Only these victims butchered at the hearth.   1310

Cassandra

There is a breath about it like an open grave.

Chorus

This is no Syrian pride of frankincense you mean.

Cassandra

So. I am going in, and mourning as I go
my death and Agamemnon's. Let my life be done.
Ah friends,   1315
truly this is no wild bird fluttering at a bush,
nor vain my speech. Bear witness to me when I die,
when falls for me, a woman slain, another woman,

and when a man dies for this wickedly mated man.
Here in my death I claim this stranger's grace of you.   1320

Chorus

Poor wretch, I pity you the fate you see so clear.

Cassandra

Yet once more will I speak, and not this time my own
death's threnody. I call upon the Sun in prayer
against that ultimate shining when the avengers strike
these monsters down in blood, that they avenge as well   1325
one simple slave who died, a small thing, lightly killed.

Alas, poor men, their destiny. When all goes well
a shadow will overthrow it. If it be unkind
one stroke of a wet sponge wipes all the picture out;
and that is far the most unhappy thing of all.   1330

                    (*Cassandra goes slowly into the house.*)

Chorus

High fortune is a thing slakeless
for mortals. There is no man who shall point
his finger to drive it back from the door
and speak the words: "Come no longer."
Now to this man the blessed ones have given   1335
Priam's city to be captured
and return in the gods' honor.
Must he give blood for generations gone,
die for those slain and in death pile up
more death to come for the blood shed,   1340
what mortal else who hears shall claim
he was born clear of the dark angel?

                    (*Agamemnon, inside the house.*)

Ah, I am struck a deadly blow and deep within!

Chorus

Silence: who cried out that he was stabbed to death within
    the house?

Agamemnon

Ah me, again, they struck again. I am wounded twice.   1345

Chorus

How the king cried out aloud to us! I believe the thing is done.
Come, let us put our heads together, try to find some safe way
out.

> (*The members of the Chorus go about distractedly,
> each one speaking in turn.*)

Listen, let me tell you what I think is best to do.
Let the herald call all citizens to rally here.

No, better to burst in upon them now, at once,   1350
and take them with the blood still running from their blades.

I am with this man and I cast my vote to him.
Act now. This is the perilous and instant time.

Anyone can see it, by these first steps they have taken,
they purpose to be tyrants here upon our city.   1355

Yes, for we waste time, while they trample to the ground
deliberation's honor, and their hands sleep not.

I can not tell which counsel of yours to call my own.
It is the man of action who can plan as well.

I feel as he does; nor can I see how by words   1360
we shall set the dead man back upon his feet again.

Do you mean, to drag our lives out long, that we must yield
to the house shamed, and leadership of such as these?

No, we can never endure that; better to be killed.
Death is a softer thing by far than tyranny.   1365

Shall we, by no more proof than that he cried in pain,
be sure, as by divination, that our lord is dead?

Yes, we should know what is true before we break our rage.
Here is sheer guessing and far different from sure knowledge.

From all sides the voices multiply to make me choose   1370
this course; to learn first how it stands with Agamemnon.

(The doors of the palace open, disclosing the bodies of
Agamemnon and Cassandra, with Clytaemestra
standing over them.)

Clytaemestra

Much have I said before to serve necessity,
but I will take no shame now to unsay it all.
How else could I, arming hate against hateful men
disguised in seeming tenderness, fence high the nets   1375
of ruin beyond overleaping? Thus to me
the conflict born of ancient bitterness is not
a thing new thought upon, but pondered deep in time.
I stand now where I struck him down. The thing is done.
Thus have I wrought, and I will not deny it now.   1380
That he might not escape nor beat aside his death,
as fishermen cast their huge circling nets, I spread
deadly abundance of rich robes, and caught him fast.
I struck him twice. In two great cries of agony
he buckled at the knees and fell. When he was down   1385
I struck him the third blow, in thanks and reverence
to Zeus the lord of dead men underneath the ground.
Thus he went down, and the life struggled out of him;
and as he died he spattered me with the dark red
and violent driven rain of bitter savored blood   1390
to make me glad, as gardens stand among the showers
of God in glory at the birthtime of the buds.

These being the facts, elders of Argos assembled here,
be glad, if it be your pleasure; but for me, I glory.
Were it religion to pour wine above the slain,   1395
this man deserved, more than deserved, such sacrament.
He filled our cup with evil things unspeakable
and now himself come home has drunk it to the dregs.

Chorus

We stand here stunned. How can you speak this way, with mouth
so arrogant, to vaunt above your fallen lord?   1400

Clytaemestra

You try me out as if I were a woman and vain;
but my heart is not fluttered as I speak before you.
You know it. You can praise or blame me as you wish;
it is all one to me. That man is Agamemnon,
my husband; he is dead; the work of this right hand   1405
that struck in strength of righteousness. And that is that.

Chorus

Woman, what evil thing planted upon the earth
or dragged from the running salt sea could you have tasted now
to wear such brutality and walk in the people's hate?
You have cast away, you have cut away. You shall go homeless
     now,   1410
crushed with men's bitterness.

Clytaemestra

Now it is I you doom to be cast out from my city
with men's hate heaped and curses roaring in my ears.
Yet look upon this dead man; you would not cross him once
when with no thought more than as if a beast had died,   1415
when his ranged pastures swarmed with the deep fleece of flocks,
he slaughtered like a victim his own child, my pain
grown into love, to charm away the winds of Thrace.
Were you not bound to hunt him then clear of this soil
for the guilt stained upon him? Yet you hear what I   1420
have done, and lo, you are a stern judge. But I say to you:
go on and threaten me, but know that I am ready,
if fairly you can beat me down beneath your hand,
for you to rule; but if the god grant otherwise,
you shall be taught—too late, for sure—to keep your place.   1425

Chorus

Great your design, your speech is a clamor of pride.
Swung to the red act drives the fury within your brain
signed clear in the splash of blood over your eyes.
Yet to come is stroke given for stroke
vengeless, forlorn of friends.   1430

Clytaemestra

> Now hear you this, the right behind my sacrament:
> By my child's Justice driven to fulfilment, by
> her Wrath and Fury, to whom I sacrificed this man,
> the hope that walks my chambers is not traced with fear
> while yet Aegisthus makes the fire shine on my hearth,   1435
> my good friend, now as always, who shall be for us
> the shield of our defiance, no weak thing; while he,
> this other, is fallen, stained with this woman you behold,
> plaything of all the golden girls at Ilium;
> and here lies she, the captive of his spear, who saw   1440
> wonders, who shared his bed, the wise in revelations
> and loving mistress, who yet knew the feel as well
> of the men's rowing benches. Their reward is not
> unworthy. He lies there; and she who swanlike cried
> aloud her lyric mortal lamentation out   1445
> is laid against his fond heart, and to me has given
> a delicate excitement to my bed's delight.

Chorus

> O that in speed, without pain
> and the slow bed of sickness
> death could come to us now, death that forever   1450
> carries sleep without ending, now that our lord is down,
> our shield, kindest of men,
> who for a woman's grace suffered so much,
> struck down at last by a woman.

> Alas, Helen, wild heart   1455
> for the multitudes, for the thousand lives
> you killed under Troy's shadow,
> you alone, to shine in man's memory
> as blood flower never to be washed out. Surely a demon then   1460
> of death walked in the house, men's agony.

Clytaemestra

> No, be not so heavy, nor yet draw down
> in prayer death's ending,

neither turn all wrath against Helen
for men dead, that she alone killed   1465
all those Danaan lives, to work
the grief that is past all healing.

Chorus

Divinity that kneel on this house and the two
strains of the blood of Tantalus,
in the hands and hearts of women you steer   1470
the strength tearing my heart.
Standing above the corpse, obscene
as some carrion crow she sings
the crippled song and is proud.

Clytaemestra

Thus have you set the speech of your lips   1475
straight, calling by name
the spirit thrice glutted that lives in this race.
From him deep in the nerve is given
the love and the blood drunk, that before
the old wound dries, it bleeds again.   1480

Chorus

Surely it is a huge
and heavy spirit bending the house you cry;
alas, the bitter glory
of a doom that shall never be done with;
and all through Zeus, Zeus,   1485
first cause, prime mover.
For what thing without Zeus is done among mortals?
What here is without God's blessing?

O king, my king
how shall I weep for you?   1490
What can I say out of my heart of pity?
Caught in this spider's web you lie,
Your life gasped out in indecent death,
struck prone to this shameful bed

by your lady's hand of treachery   1495
and the stroke twin edged of the iron.

Clytaemestra

Can you claim I have done this?
Speak of me never
more as the wife of Agamemnon.
In the shadow of this corpse's queen   1500
the old stark avenger
of Atreus for his revel of hate
struck down this man,
last blood for the slaughtered children.

Chorus

What man shall testify   1505
your hands are clean of this murder?
How? How? Yet from his father's blood
might swarm some fiend to guide you.
The black ruin that shoulders
through the streaming blood of brothers   1510
strides at last where he shall win requital
for the children who were eaten.

O king, my king
how shall I weep for you?
What can I say out of my heart of pity?   1515
Caught in this spider's web you lie,
your life gasped out in indecent death,
struck prone to this shameful bed
by your lady's hand of treachery
and the stroke twin edged of the iron.   1520

Clytaemestra

No shame, I think, in the death given
this man. And did he not
first of all in this house wreak death
by treachery?
The flower of this man's love and mine,   1525

Iphigeneia of the tears
he dealt with even as he has suffered.
Let his speech in death's house be not loud.
With the sword he struck,
with the sword he paid for his own act.

Chorus

My thoughts are swept away and I go bewildered.   1530
Where shall I turn the brain's
activity in speed when the house is falling?
There is fear in the beat of the blood rain breaking
wall and tower. The drops come thicker.
Still fate grinds on yet more stones the blade   1535
for more acts of terror.

Earth, my earth, why did you not fold me under
before ever I saw this man lie dead
fenced by the tub in silver?   1540
Who shall bury him? Who shall mourn him?
Shall you dare this who have killed
your lord? Make lamentation,
render the graceless grace to his soul   1545
for huge things done in wickedness?
Who over this great man's grave shall lay
the blessing of tears
worked soberly from a true heart?   1550

Clytaemestra

Not for you to speak of such tendance.
Through us he fell,
by us he died; we shall bury.
There will be no tears in this house for him.
It must be Iphigeneia   1555
his child, who else,
shall greet her father by the whirling stream
and the ferry of tears
to close him in her arms and kiss him.

Chorus

> Here is anger for anger. Between them   1560
> who shall judge lightly?
> The spoiler is robbed; he killed, he has paid.
> The truth stands ever beside God's throne
> eternal: he who has wrought shall pay; that is law.
> Then who shall tear the curse from their blood?   1565
> The seed is stiffened to ruin.

Clytaemestra

> You see truth in the future
> at last. Yet I wish
> to seal my oath with the Spirit
> in the house: I will endure all things as they stand   1570
> now, hard though it be. Hereafter
> let him go forth to make bleed with death
> and guilt the houses of others.
> I will take some small
> measure of our riches, and be content
> that I swept from these halls   1575
> the murder, the sin, and the fury.

> *(Aegisthus enters, followed at a little distance by his*
> *armed bodyguard.)*

Aegisthus

> O splendor and exaltation of this day of doom!
> Now I can say once more that the high gods look down
> on mortal crimes to vindicate the right at last,
> now that I see this man—sweet sight—before me here   1580
> sprawled in the tangling nets of fury, to atone
> the calculated evil of his father's hand.
> For Atreus, this man's father, King of Argolis—
> I tell you the clear story—drove my father forth,
> Thyestes, his own brother, who had challenged him   1585
> in his king's right—forth from his city and his home.
> Yet sad Thyestes came again to supplicate
> the hearth, and win some grace, in that he was not slain

nor soiled the doorstone of his fathers with blood spilled.
Not his own blood. But Atreus, this man's godless sire,   1590
angrily hospitable set a feast for him,
in seeming a glad day of fresh meat slain and good
cheer; then served my father his own children's flesh
to feed on. For he carved away the extremities,
hands, feet, and cut the flesh apart, and covered them   1595
served in a dish to my father at his table apart,
who with no thought for the featureless meal before him ate
that ghastly food whose curse works now before your eyes.
But when he knew the terrible thing that he had done,
he spat the dead meat from him with a cry, and reeled   1600
spurning the table back to heel with strength the curse:
"Thus crash in ruin all the seed of Pleisthenes."
Out of such acts you see this dead man stricken here,
and it was I, in my right, who wrought this murder, I
third born to my unhappy father, and with him   1605
driven, a helpless baby in arms, to banishment.
Yet I grew up, and justice brought me home again,
till from afar I laid my hands upon this man,
since it was I who pieced together the fell plot.
Now I can die in honor again, if die I must,   1610
having seen him caught in the cords of his just punishment.

Chorus

Aegisthus, this strong vaunting in distress is vile,
You claim that you deliberately killed the king,
you, and you only, wrought the pity of this death.
I tell you then: There shall be no escape, your head   1615
shall face the stones of anger from the people's hands.

Aegisthus

So loud from you, stooped to the meanest rowing bench
with the ship's masters lordly on the deck above?
You are old men; well, you shall learn how hard it is
at your age, to be taught how to behave yourselves.   1620
But there are chains, there is starvation with its pain,

excellent teachers of good manners to old men,
wise surgeons and exemplars. Look! Can you not see it?
Lash not at the goads for fear you hit them, and be hurt.

Chorus

So then you, like a woman, waited the war out   1625
here in the house, shaming the master's bed with lust,
and planned against the lord of war this treacherous death?

Aegisthus

It is just such words as these will make you cry in pain.
Not yours the lips of Orpheus, no, quite otherwise,
whose voice of rapture dragged all creatures in his train.   1630
You shall be dragged, for baby whimperings sobbed out
in rage. Once broken, you will be easier to deal with.

Chorus

How shall you be lord of the men of Argos, you
who planned the murder of this man, yet could not dare
to act it out, and cut him down with your own hand?   1635

Aegisthus

No, clearly the deception was the woman's part,
and I was suspect, that had hated him so long.
Still with his money I shall endeavor to control
the citizens. The mutinous man shall feel the yoke
drag at his neck, no cornfed racing colt that runs   1640
free traced; but hunger, grim companion of the dark
dungeon shall see him broken to the hand at last.

Chorus

But why, why then, you coward, could you not have slain
your man yourself? Why must it be his wife who killed,
to curse the country and the gods within the ground?   1645
Oh, can Orestes live, be somewhere in sunlight still?
Shall fate grown gracious ever bring him back again
in strength of hand to overwhelm these murderers?

Aegisthus

You shall learn then, since you stick to stubbornness of mouth
and hand.

Up now from your cover, my henchmen: here is work for you
to do.   1650

Chorus

Look, they come! Let every man clap fist upon his hilted sword.

Aegisthus

I too am sword-handed against you; I am not afraid of death.

Chorus

Death you said and death it shall be; we take up the word of
fate.

Clytaemestra

No, my dearest, dearest of all men, we have done enough. No
more

violence. Here is a monstrous harvest and a bitter reaping time.   1655
There is pain enough already. Let us not be bloody now.
Honored gentlemen of Argos, go to your homes now and give
way

to the stress of fate and season. We could not do otherwise
than we did. If this is the end of suffering, we can be content
broken as we are by the brute heel of angry destiny.   1660
Thus a woman speaks among you. Shall men deign to under-
stand?

Aegisthus

Yes, but think of these foolish lips that blossom into leering gibes,
think of the taunts they spit against me daring destiny and power,
sober opinion lost in insults hurled against my majesty.

Chorus

It was never the Argive way to grovel at a vile man's feet.   1665

Aegisthus

I shall not forget this; in the days to come I shall be there.

Chorus

Nevermore, if God's hand guiding brings Orestes home again.

Aegisthus

Exiles feed on empty dreams of hope. I know it. I was one.

Chorus

Have your way, gorge and grow fat, soil justice, while the power is yours.

Aegisthus

You shall pay, make no mistake, for this misguided insolence.   1670

Chorus

Crow and strut, brave cockerel by your hen; you have no threats to fear.

Clytaemestra

These are howls of impotent rage; forget them, dearest; you and I

have the power; we two shall bring good order to our house at least.

(*They enter the house. The doors close. All persons leave the stage.*)

PROMETHEUS BOUND

Translated by David Grene

INTRODUCTION

The date of this play is unknown. The other two tragedies which completed the trilogy are lost, and the arrangement is disputed. I give here the reconstruction which seems most plausible to me.

Prometheus Bound is the first play in the trilogy. It opens, of course, with the fastening of Prometheus to the rock, but a great deal of the body of the play is taken up with the explanation, through the hero's conversations with others, of how this punishment has come about. In the great revolution of the Olympians against their elders, the Titans, Prometheus, a Titan, went over to the side of the Olympians; it is, he claims, thanks to him that Olympian Zeus is now the master of the universe. But Prometheus outraged Zeus by befriending, against the plans of Zeus, the pitiful, rudimentary, experimental race of men. Therefore he is punished and, at the end, sunk beneath the earth, whence he will emerge only to face the new torment of the bird of prey which will feed upon his liver. The sequel, *Prometheus Unbound*, of which some fragments remain, would find Prometheus in his new agony. Heracles, the descendant of Io, frees him by killing the eagle. But his final reconciliation with Zeus, confidently predicted in *Prometheus Bound*, must be deferred to the totally lost *Prometheus the Firebearer*, last of the trilogy, which would end in his installation as a god of cult and the establishment of the ritual torch race which is partly in his honor.

The startling fact about *Prometheus Bound* is the cruel, almost villainous part played by Zeus. Although he never appears, his motives seem plain, and they are those of a tyrant. Romantic poets such as Goethe and Shelley welcomed this story as a parable of human revolt against autocracy and established religion. Others, seeing Aeschylus as a pious conservative, an awe-struck Zeus-man, have sometimes been so troubled as to deny that Aeschylus wrote the play at all. It is better to consider the drama, within its trilogy, not as a piece of theology but as a play, a story, using superhuman materials. For Prometheus, though overpowered, is a full immortal god, not a man. This use of an omniscient indestructible deity in place of the faulted human hero presents its dramatic difficulties. It makes the action static. But the ultimate reconciliation is not to be forgotten.

CHARACTERS

Might

Violence (muta persona)

Hephaestus

Prometheus

Oceanos

Io

Hermes

Chorus of daughters of Oceanos

PROMETHEUS BOUND

SCENE: *A bare and desolate crag in the Caucasus. Enter Might and*
Violence, demons, servants of Zeus, and Hephaestus, the smith.

Might

This is the world's limit that we have come to; this is the Scythian
country, an untrodden desolation. Hephaestus, it is you that must
heed the commands the Father laid upon you to nail this malefac-
tor to the high craggy rocks in fetters unbreakable of adamantine
chain. For it was your flower, the brightness of fire that devises
all, that he stole and gave to mortal men; this is the sin for which
he must pay the Gods the penalty—that he may learn to endure   10
and like the sovereignty of Zeus and quit his man-loving disposition.

Hephaestus

Might and Violence, in you the command of Zeus has its perfect
fulfilment: in you there is nothing to stand in its way. But, for
myself, I have not the heart to bind violently a God who is my kin
here on this wintry cliff. Yet there is constraint upon me to have
the heart for just that, for it is a dangerous thing to treat the
Father's words lightly.

High-contriving Son of Themis of Straight Counsel: this is not of
your will nor of mine; yet I shall nail you in bonds of indissoluble
bronze on this crag far from men. Here you shall hear no voice   20
of mortal; here you shall see no form of mortal. You shall be
grilled by the sun's bright fire and change the fair bloom of your
skin. You shall be glad when Night comes with her mantle of
stars and hides the sun's light; but the sun shall scatter the hoar-
frost again at dawn. Always the grievous burden of your torture
will be there to wear you down; for he that shall cause it to cease
has yet to be born.

Such is the reward you reap of your man-loving disposition. For you, a God, feared not the anger of the Gods, but gave honors to mortals beyond what was just. Wherefore you shall mount guard on this unlovely rock, upright, sleepless, not bending the knee. Many a groan and many a lamentation you shall utter, but they shall not serve you. For the mind of Zeus is hard to soften with prayer, and every ruler is harsh whose rule is new.

Might

Come, why are you holding back? Why are you pitying in vain? Why is it that you do not hate a God whom the Gods hate most of all? Why do you not hate him, since it was your honor that he betrayed to men?

Hephaestus

Our kinship has strange power; that, and our life together.

Might

Yes. But to turn a deaf ear to the Father's words—how can that be? Do you not fear that more?

Hephaestus

You are always pitiless, always full of ruthlessness.

Might

There is no good singing dirges over him. Do not labor uselessly at what helps not at all.

Hephaestus

O handicraft of mine—that I deeply hate!

Might

Why do you hate it? To speak simply, your craft is in no way the author of his present troubles.

Hephaestus

Yet would another had had this craft allotted to him.

Might

There is nothing without discomfort except the overlordship of the Gods. For only Zeus is free.

Hephaestus

I know. I have no answer to this.

Might

Hurry now. Throw the chain around him that the Father may not
look upon your tarrying.

Hephaestus

There are the fetters, there: you can see them.

Might

Put them on his hands: strong, now with the hammer: strike.
Nail him to the rock.

Hephaestus

It is being done now. I am not idling at my work.

Might

Hammer it more; put in the wedge; leave it loose nowhere. He's a
cunning fellow at finding a way even out of hopeless difficulties

Hephaestus

Look now, his arm is fixed immovably!   60

Might

Nail the other safe, that he may learn, for all his cleverness, that
he is duller witted than Zeus.

Hephaestus

No one, save Prometheus, can justly blame me.

Might

Drive the obstinate jaw of the adamantine wedge right through
his breast: drive it hard.

Hephaestus

Alas, Prometheus, I groan for your sufferings.

Might

Are you pitying again? Are you groaning for the enemies of
Zeus? Have a care, lest some day you may be pitying yourself.

Hephaestus

You see a sight that hurts the eye.

Might

I see this rascal getting his deserts. Throw the girth around his   70
sides.

Hephaestus

I am forced to do this; do not keep urging me.

Might

Yes, I will urge you, and hound you on as well. Get below now, and hoop his legs in strongly.

Hephaestus

There now, the task is done. It has not taken long.

Might

Hammer the piercing fetters with all your power, for the Overseer of our work is severe.

Hephaestus

Your looks and the refrain of your tongue are alike.

Might

You can be softhearted. But do not blame my stubbornness and harshness of temper.   80

Hephaestus

Let us go. He has the harness on his limbs.

Might (to Prometheus)

Now, play the insolent; now, plunder the Gods' privileges and give them to creatures of a day. What drop of your sufferings can mortals spare you? The Gods named you wrongly when they called you Forethought; you yourself *need* Forethought to extricate yourself from this contrivance.

(Prometheus is left alone on the rock.)

Prometheus

Bright light, swift-winged winds, springs of the rivers, numberless
laughter of the sea's waves, earth, mother of all, and the all-seeing   90
circle of the sun: I call upon you to see what I, a God, suffer
at the hands of Gods—
see with what kind of torture
worn down I shall wrestle ten thousand
years of time—

such is the despiteful bond that the Prince
has devised against me, the new Prince
of the Blessed Ones. Oh woe is me!
I groan for the present sorrow,
I groan for the sorrow to come, I groan
questioning when there shall come a time
when He shall ordain a limit to my sufferings.
What am I saying? I have known all before,   100
all that shall be, and clearly known; to me,
nothing that hurts shall come with a new face.
So must I bear, as lightly as I can,
the destiny that fate has given me;
for I know well against necessity,
against its strength, no one can fight and win.

I cannot speak about my fortune, cannot
hold my tongue either. It was mortal man
to whom I gave great privileges and
for that was yoked in this unyielding harness.
I hunted out the secret spring of fire,
that filled the narthex stem, which when revealed   110
became the teacher of each craft to men,
a great resource. This is the sin committed
for which I stand accountant, and I pay
nailed in my chains under the open sky.

Ah! Ah!
What sound, what sightless smell approaches me,
God sent, or mortal, or mingled?
Has it come to earth's end
to look on my sufferings,
or what does it wish?
You see me a wretched God in chains,   120
the enemy of Zeus, hated of all
the Gods that enter Zeus's palace hall,
because of my excessive love for Man.

What is that? The rustle
of birds' wings near? The air whispers
with the gentle strokes of wings.
Everything that comes toward me is occasion for fear.

> (*The Chorus, composed of the daughters of Oceanos, enters,*
> *the members wearing some formalized representation of*
> *wings, so that their general appearance is birdlike.*)

Chorus

Fear not: this is a company of friends
that comes to your mountain with swift
rivalry of wings.   130
Hardly have we persuaded our Father's
mind, and the quick-bearing winds
speeded us hither. The sound
of stroke of bronze rang through our cavern
in its depths and it shook from us
shamefaced modesty; unsandaled
we have hastened on our chariot of wings.

Prometheus

Alas, children of teeming Tethys and of him
who encircles all the world with stream unsleeping,
Father Ocean,   140
look, see with what chains
I am nailed on the craggy heights
of this gully to keep a watch
that none would envy me.

Chorus

I see, Prometheus: and a mist of fear and tears
besets my eyes as I see your form
wasting away on these cliffs
in adamantine bonds of bitter shame.
For new are the steersmen that rule Olympus:
and new are the customs by which Zeus rules,
customs that have no law to them,   150
but what was great before he brings to nothingness.

Prometheus

Would that he had hurled me
underneath the earth and underneath
the House of Hades, host to the dead—
yes, down to limitless Tartarus,
yes, though he bound me cruelly
in chains unbreakable,
so neither God nor any other being
might have found joy in gloating over me.
Now as I hang, the plaything of the winds,
my enemies can laugh at what I suffer.

Chorus

Who of the Gods is so hard of heart   160
that he finds joy in this?
Who is that that does not feel
sorrow answering your pain—
save only Zeus? For he malignantly,
always cherishing a mind
that bends not, has subdued the breed
of Uranos, nor shall he cease
until he satisfies his heart,
or someone take the rule from him—that hard-to-capture rule—
by some device of subtlety.

Prometheus

Yes, there shall come a day for me
when he shall need me, me that now am tortured
in bonds and fetters—he shall need me then,
this president of the Blessed—   170
to show the new plot whereby he may be spoiled
of his throne and his power.
Then not with honeyed tongues
of persuasion shall he enchant me;
he shall not cow me with his threats
to tell him what I know,

until he free me from my cruel chains
and pay me recompense for what I suffer.

Chorus

You are stout of heart, unyielding   180
to the bitterness of pain.
You are free of tongue, too free.
It is my mind that piercing fear has fluttered;
your misfortunes frighten me.
Where and when is it fated
to see you reach the term, to see you reach
the harbor free of trouble at the last?
A disposition none can win, a heart
that no persuasions soften—these are his,
the Son of Kronos.

Prometheus

I know that he is savage: and his justice
a thing he keeps by his own standard: still
that will of his shall melt to softness yet   190
when he is broken in the way I know,
and though his temper now is oaken hard
it shall be softened: hastily he'll come
to meet my haste, to join in amity
and union with me—one day he shall come.

Chorus

Reveal it all to us: tell us the story of what the charge was on
which Zeus caught you and punished you so cruelly with such dishonor. Tell us, if the telling will not injure you in any way.

Prometheus

To speak of this is bitterness. To keep silent
bitter no less; and every way is misery.   200

When first the Gods began their angry quarrel,
and God matched God in rising faction, some
eager to drive old Kronos from his throne
that Zeus might rule—the fools!—others again

earnest that Zeus might never be their king—
I then with the best counsel tried to win
the Titans, sons of Uranos and Earth,
but failed. They would have none of crafty schemes
and in their savage arrogance of spirit
thought they would lord it easily by force.   210
But she that was my mother, Themis, Earth—
she is but one although her names are many—
had prophesied to me how it should be,
even how the fates decreed it: and she said
that "not by strength nor overmastering force
the fates allowed the conquerors to conquer
but by guile only": This is what I told them,
but they would not vouchsafe a glance at me.
Then with those things before me it seemed best
to take my mother and join Zeus's side: 220
he was as willing as we were:
thanks to my plans the dark receptacle
of Tartarus conceals the ancient Kronos,
him and his allies. These were the services
I rendered to this tyrant and these pains
the payment he has given me in requital.
This is a sickness rooted and inherent
in the nature of a tyranny:
that he that holds it does not trust his friends.

But you have asked on what particular
charge he now tortures me: this I will tell you.
As soon as he ascended to the throne   230
that was his father's, straightway he assigned
to the several Gods their several privileges
and portioned out the power, but to the unhappy
breed of mankind he gave no heed, intending
to blot the race out and create a new.
Against these plans none stood save I: I dared.

I rescued men from shattering destruction
that would have carried them to Hades' house;
and therefore I am tortured on this rock,
a bitterness to suffer, and a pain
to pitiful eyes. I gave to mortal man   240
a precedence over myself in pity: I
can win no pity: pitiless is he
that thus chastises me, a spectacle
bringing dishonor on the name of Zeus.

Chorus

He would be iron-minded and made of stone, indeed, Prometheus, who did not sympathize with your sufferings. I would not
have chosen to see them, and now that I see, my heart is pained.

Prometheus

Yes, to my friends I am pitiable to see.

Chorus

Did you perhaps go further than you have told us?

Prometheus

I caused mortals to cease foreseeing doom.   250

Chorus

What cure did you provide them with against that sickness?

Prometheus

I placed in them blind hopes.

Chorus

That was a great gift you gave to men.

Prometheus

Besides this, I gave them fire.

Chorus

And do creatures of a day now possess bright-faced fire?

Prometheus

Yes, and from it they shall learn many crafts.

Chorus

Then these are the charges on which—

Prometheus

Zeus tortures me and gives me no respite.

Chorus

Is there no limit set for your pain?

Prometheus

None save when it shall seem good to Zeus.   260

Chorus

How will it ever seem good to him? What hope is there? Do you
not see how you have erred? It is not pleasure for me to say that
you have erred, and for you it is a pain to hear. But let us speak no
more of all this and do you seek some means of deliverance from
your trials.

Prometheus

It is an easy thing for one whose foot
is on the outside of calamity
to give advice and to rebuke the sufferer.
I have known all that you have said: I knew,
I knew when I transgressed nor will deny it.
In helping man I brought my troubles on me;
but yet I did not think that with such tortures   270
I should be wasted on these airy cliffs,
this lonely mountain top, with no one near.
But do not sorrow for my present suffering;
alight on earth and hear what is to come
that you may know the whole complete: I beg you
alight and join your sorrow with mine: misfortune
wandering the same track lights now upon one
and now upon another.

Chorus

                    Willing our ears,
that hear you cry to them, Prometheus,   280
now with light foot I leave the rushing car
and sky, the holy path of birds, and light
upon this jutting rock: I long
to hear your story to the end.

                (Enter Oceanos, riding on a hippocamp, or sea-monster.)

Oceanos

                  I come
on a long journey, speeding past the boundaries,
to visit you, Prometheus: with the mind
alone, no bridle needed, I direct
my swift-winged bird; my heart is sore
for your misfortunes; you know that. I think   290
that it is kinship makes me feel them so.
Besides, apart from kinship, there is no one
I hold in higher estimation: that
you soon shall know and know beside that in me
there is no mere word-kindness: tell me
how I can help you, and you will never say
that you have any friend more loyal to you
than Oceanos.

Prometheus

What do I see? Have you, too, come to gape   300
in wonder at this great display, my torture?
How did you have the courage to come here
to this land, Iron-Mother, leaving the stream
called after you and the rock-roofed, self-established
caverns? Was it to feast your eyes upon
the spectacle of my suffering and join
in pity for my pain? Now look and see
the sight, this friend of Zeus, that helped set up
his tyranny and see what agonies
twist me, by his instructions!

Oceanos

                Yes, I see,
Prometheus, and I want, indeed I do,
to advise you for the best, for all your cleverness.   310
Know yourself and reform your ways to new ways,
for new is he that rules among the Gods.
But if you throw about such angry words,

words that are whetted swords, soon Zeus will hear you,
even though his seat in glory is far removed,
and then your present multitude of pains
will seem like child's play. My poor friend, give up
this angry mood of yours and look for means
of getting yourself free of trouble. Maybe
what I say seems to you both old and commonplace;
but this is what you pay, Prometheus, for   320
that tongue of yours which talked so high and haughty:
you are not yet humble, still you do not yield
to your misfortunes, and you wish, indeed,
to add some more to them; now, if you follow
me as a schoolmaster you will not kick
against the pricks, seeing that he, the King,
that rules alone, is harsh and sends accounts
to no one's audit for the deeds he does.
Now I will go and try if I can free you:
do you be quiet, do not talk so much.
Since your mind is so subtle, don't you know   330
that a vain tongue is subject to correction?

Prometheus

  I envy you, that you stand clear of blame,
yet shared and dared in everything with me!
Now let me be, and have no care for me.
Do what you will, Him you will not persuade;
He is not easily won over: look,
take care lest coming here to me should hurt you.

Oceanos

  You are by nature better at advising
others than yourself. I take my cue
from deeds, not words. Do not withhold me now
when I am eager to go to Zeus. I'm sure,
I'm sure that he will grant this favor to me,   340
to free you from your chains.

Prometheus

I thank you and will never cease; for loyalty
is not what you are wanting in. Don't trouble,
for you will trouble to no purpose, and no help
to me—if it so be you want to trouble.
No, rest yourself, keep away from this thing;
because I am unlucky I would not,
for that, have everyone unlucky too.
No, for my heart is sore already when
I think about my brothers' fortunes—Atlas,   350
who stands to westward of the world, supporting
the pillar of earth and heaven on his shoulders,
a load that suits no shoulders; and the earthborn
dweller in caves Cilician, whom I saw
and pitied, hundred-headed, dreadful monster,
fierce Typho, conquered and brought low by force.
Once against all the Gods he stood, opposing,
hissing out terror from his grim jaws; his eyes
flashed gorgon glaring lightning as he thought
to sack the sovereign tyranny of Zeus;
but upon him came the unsleeping bolt
of Zeus, the lightning-breathing flame, down rushing,   360
which cast him from his high aspiring boast.
Struck to the heart, his strength was blasted dead
and burnt to ashes; now a sprawling mass
useless he lies, hard by the narrow seaway
pressed down beneath the roots of Aetna: high
above him on the mountain peak the smith
Hephaestus works at the anvil. Yet one day
there shall burst out rivers of fire, devouring
with savage jaws the fertile, level plains   370
of Sicily of the fair fruits; such boiling wrath
with weapons of fire-breathing surf, a fiery
unapproachable torrent, shall Typho vomit,
though Zeus's lightning left him but a cinder.

But all of this you know: you do not need me
to be your schoolmaster: reassure yourself
as you know how: this cup I shall drain myself
till the high mind of Zeus shall cease from anger.

Oceanos

Do you not know, Prometheus, that words are healers of the
sick temper?   380

Prometheus

Yes, if in season due one soothes the heart with them, not tries
violently to reduce the swelling anger.

Oceanos

Tell me, what danger do you see for me in loyalty to you, and
courage therein?

Prometheus

I see only useless effort and a silly good nature.

Oceanos

Suffer me then to be sick of this sickness, for it is a profitable
thing, if one is wise, to seem foolish.

Prometheus

This shall seem to be my fault.

Oceanos

Clearly your words send me home again.

Prometheus

Yes, lest your doings for me bring you enmity.   390

Oceanos

His enmity, who newly sits on the all-powerful throne?

Prometheus

His is a heart you should beware of vexing.

Oceanos

Your own misfortune will be my teacher, Prometheus.

Prometheus

Off with you, then! Begone! Keep your present mind.

Oceanos

These words fall on very responsive ears. Already my four-legged bird is pawing the level track of Heaven with his wings, and he will be glad to bend the knee in his own stable.

Chorus

STROPHE

I cry aloud, Prometheus, and lament your bitter fate,
my tender eyes are trickling tears: 400
their fountains wet my cheek.
This is a tyrant's deed; this is unlovely,
a thing done by a tyrant's private laws,
and with this thing Zeus shows his haughtiness
of temper toward the Gods that were of old.

ANTISTROPHE

Now all the earth has cried aloud, lamenting:
now all that was magnificent of old
laments your fall, laments your brethren's fall   410
as many as in holy Asia hold
their stablished habitation, all lament
in sympathy for your most grievous woes.

STROPHE

Dwellers in the land of Colchis,
maidens, fearless in the fight,
and the host of Scythia, living
round the lake Maeotis, living
on the edges of the world.

ANTISTROPHE

And Arabia's flower of warriors   420
and the craggy fortress keepers
near Caucasian mountains, fighters
terrible, crying for battle,
brandishing sharp pointed spears.

STROPHE

One God and one God only I have seen
before this day, in torture and in bonds
unbreakable: he was a Titan,
Alas, whose strength and might
ever exceeded; now he bends his back
and groans beneath the load of earth and heaven. 430

ANTISTROPHE

The wave cries out as it breaks into surf;
the depth cries out, lamenting you; the dark
Hades, the hollow underneath the world,
sullenly groans below; the springs
of sacred flowing rivers all lament
the pain and pity of your suffering.

Prometheus

Do not think that out of pride or stubbornness I hold my peace;
my heart is eaten away when I am aware of myself, when I see
myself insulted as I am. Who was it but I who in truth dispensed
their honors to these new gods? I will say nothing of this; you 440
know it all; but hear what troubles there were among men, how
I found them witless and gave them the use of their wits and made
them masters of their minds. I will tell you this, not because I
would blame men, but to explain the goodwill of my gift. For
men at first had eyes but saw to no purpose; they had ears but did
not hear. Like the shapes of dreams they dragged through their
long lives and handled all things in bewilderment and confusion.
They did not know of building houses with bricks to face the sun;
they did not know how to work in wood. They lived like swarm-
ing ants in holes in the ground, in the sunless caves of the earth. 450
For them there was no secure token by which to tell winter nor
the flowering spring nor the summer with its crops; all their doings were indeed without intelligent calculation until I showed
them the rising of the stars, and the settings, hard to observe. And
further I discovered to them numbering, pre-eminent among

subtle devices, and the combining of letters as a means of re-membering all things, the Muses' mother, skilled in craft. It was I who first yoked beasts for them in the yokes and made of those beasts the slaves of trace chain and pack saddle that they might be man's substitute in the hardest tasks; and I harnessed to the carriage, so that they loved the rein, horses, the crowning pride of the rich man's luxury. It was I and none other who discovered ships, the sail-driven wagons that the sea buffets. Such were the contrivances that I discovered for men—alas for me! For I myself am without contrivance to rid myself of my present affliction.

Chorus

What you have suffered is indeed terrible. You are all astray and bewildered in your mind, and like a bad doctor that has fallen sick himself, you are cast down and cannot find what sort of drugs would cure your ailment.

Prometheus

Hear the rest, and you will marvel even more at the crafts and resources I contrived. Greatest was this: in the former times if a man fell sick he had no defense against the sickness, neither healing food nor drink, nor unguent; but through the lack of drugs men wasted away, until I showed them the blending of mild simples wherewith they drive out all manner of diseases. It was I who arranged all the ways of seercraft, and I first adjudged what things come verily true from dreams; and to men I gave meaning to the ominous cries, hard to interpret. It was I who set in order the omens of the highway and the flight of crooked-taloned birds, which of them were propitious or lucky by nature, and what manner of life each led, and what were their mutual hates, loves, and companionships; also I taught of the smoothness of the vitals and what color they should have to pleasure the Gods and the dappled beauty of the gall and the lobe. It was I who burned thighs wrapped in fat and the long shank bone and set mortals on the road to this murky craft. It was I who made visible to men's eyes the flaming signs of the sky that were

460

470

480

490

before dim. So much for these. Beneath the earth, man's hidden
blessing, copper, iron, silver, and gold—will anyone claim to
have discovered these before I did? No one, I am very sure, who
wants to speak truly and to the purpose. One brief word will tell
the whole story: all arts that mortals have come from Prometheus. 500

Chorus

Therefore do not help mortals beyond all expediency while neg-
lecting yourself in your troubles. For I am of good hope that once
freed of these bonds you will be no less in power than Zeus. 510

Prometheus

Not yet has fate that brings to fulfilment determined these things
to be thus. I must be twisted by ten thousand pangs and agonies,
as I now am, to escape my chains at last. Craft is far weaker than
necessity.

Chorus

Who then is the steersman of necessity?

Prometheus

The triple-formed Fates and the remembering Furies.

Chorus

Is Zeus weaker than these?

Prometheus

Yes, for he, too, cannot escape what is fated.

Chorus

What is fated for Zeus besides eternal sovereignty?

Prometheus

Inquire of this no further, do not entreat me. 520

Chorus

This is some solemn secret, I suppose, that you are hiding.

Prometheus

Think of some other story: this one it is not yet the season to give
tongue to, but it must be hidden with all care; for it is only by
keeping it that I will escape my despiteful bondage and my agony.

Chorus

May Zeus never, Zeus that all
the universe controls, oppose
his power against my mind:
may I never dallying
be slow to give my worship at
the sacrificial feasts
when the bulls are killed beside
quenchless Father Ocean:
may I never sin in word:
may these precepts still abide
in my mind nor melt away.

ANTISTROPHE

It is a sweet thing to draw out
a long, long life in cheerful hopes,
and feed the spirit in the bright
benignity of happiness:
but I shiver when I see you
wasted with ten thousand pains,
all because you did not tremble
at the name of Zeus: your mind
was yours, not his, and at its bidding
you regarded mortal men
too high, Prometheus.

STROPHE

Kindness that cannot be requited, tell me,
where is the help in that, my friend? What succor
in creatures of a day? You did not see
the feebleness that draws its breath in gasps,
a dreamlike feebleness by which the race
of man is held in bondage, a blind prisoner.
So the plans of men shall never
pass the ordered law of Zeus.

530

540

550

ANTISTROPHE

This I have learned while I looked on your pains,
deadly pains, Prometheus.
A dirge for you came to my lips, so different
from the other song I sang to crown your marriage
in honor of your couching and your bath,
upon the day you won her with your gifts
to share your bed—of your own race she was,
Hesione—and so you brought her home.   560

(Enter Io, a girl wearing horns like an ox.)

Io

What land is this? what race of men? Who is it
I see here tortured in this rocky bondage?
What is the sin he's paying for? Oh tell me
to what part of the world my wanderings have brought me.
O, O, O,
there it is again, there again—it stings me,
the gadfly, the ghost of earth-born Argos:
keep it away, keep it away, earth!
I'm frightened when I see the shape of Argos,
Argos the herdsman with ten thousand eyes.   570
He stalks me with his crafty eyes: he died,
but the earth didn't hide him; still he comes
even from the depths of the Underworld to hunt me:
he drives me starving by the sands of the sea.

The reed-woven pipe drones on in a hum
and drones and drones its sleep-giving strain:
O, O, O,
Where are you bringing me, my far-wandering wanderings?
Son of Kronos, what fault, what fault
did you find in me that you should yoke me
to a harness of misery like this,
that you should torture me so to madness   580
driven in fear of the gadfly?

Burn me with fire: hide me in earth: cast me away
to monsters of the deep for food: but do not
grudge me the granting of this prayer, King.
Enough have my much wandering wanderings
exercised me: I cannot find
a way to escape my troubles.
Do you hear the voice of the cow-horned maid?

Prometheus

Surely I hear the voice, the voice of the maiden, gadfly-haunted,
the daughter of Inachus? She set Zeus's heart on fire with love   590
and now she is violently exercised running on courses overlong,
driven by Hera's hate.

Io

How is it you speak my father's name?
Tell me, who are you? Who are you? Oh
who are you that so exactly accosts me by name?
You have spoken of the disease that the Gods have sent to me
which wastes me away, pricking with goads,
so that I am moving always
tortured and hungry, wild bounding,
quick sped I come,   600
a victim of jealous plots.
Some have been wretched
before me, but who of these
suffered as I do?
But declare to me clearly
what I have still to suffer: what would avail
against my sickness, what drug would cure it:
Tell me, if you know:
tell me, declare it to the unlucky, wandering maid.

Prometheus

I shall tell you clearly all that you would know, weaving you no
riddles, but in plain words, as it is just to open the lips to friends.   610
You see before you him that gave fire to men, even Prometheus.

Io

O spirit that has appeared as a common blessing to all men, unhappy Prometheus, why are you being punished?

Prometheus

I have just this moment ceased from the lamentable tale of my sorrows.

Io

Will you then grant me this favor?

Prometheus

Say what you are asking for: I will tell you all.

Io

Tell who it was that nailed you to the cliff.

Prometheus

The plan was the plan of Zeus, and the hand the hand of Hephaestus.

Io

And what was the offense of which this is the punishment?   620

Prometheus

It is enough that I have told you a clear story so far.

Io

In addition, then, indicate to me what date shall be the limit of my wanderings.

Prometheus

Better for you not to know this than know it.

Io

I beg you, do not hide from me what I must endure.

Prometheus

It is not that I grudge you this favor.

Io

Why then delay to tell me all?

Prometheus

It is no grudging, but I hesitate to break your spirit.

Io

Do not have more thought for me than pleases me myself.

Prometheus

Since you are so eager, I must speak; and do you give ear.   630

Chorus

Not yet: give me, too, a share of pleasure. First let us question her concerning her sickness, and let her tell us of her desperate fortunes. And then let you be our informant for the sorrows that still await her.

Prometheus

It is your task, Io, to gratify these spirits, for besides other considerations they are your father's sisters. To make wail and lament for one's ill fortune, when one will win a tear from the audience, is well worthwhile.

Io

I know not how I should distrust you: clearly   640
you shall hear all you want to know from me.
Yet even as I speak I groan in bitterness
for that storm sent by God on me, that ruin
of my beauty; I must sorrow when I think
who sent all this upon me. There were always
night visions that kept haunting me and coming
into my maiden chamber and exhorting
with winning words, "O maiden greatly blessed,
why are you still a maiden, you who might
make marriage with the greatest? Zeus is stricken
with lust for you; he is afire to try   650
the bed of love with you: do not disdain him.
Go, child, to Lerna's meadow, deep in grass,
to where your father's flocks and cattle stand
that Zeus's eye may cease from longing for you."
With such dreams I was cruelly beset
night after night until I took the courage
to tell my father of my nightly terror.

He sent to Pytho many an embassy
and to Dodona seeking to discover
what deed or word of his might please the God,   660
but those he sent came back with riddling oracles
dark and beyond the power of understanding.
At last the word came clear to Inachus
charging him plainly that he cast me out
of home and country, drive me out footloose
to wander to the limits of the world;
if he should not obey, the oracle said,
the fire-faced thunderbolt would come from Zeus
and blot out his whole race. These were the oracles
of Loxias, and Inachus obeyed them.   670
He drove me out and shut his doors against me
with tears on both our parts, but Zeus's bit
compelled him to do this against his will.
Immediately my form and mind were changed
and all distorted; horned, as you see,
pricked on by the sharp biting gadfly, leaping
in frenzied jumps I ran beside the river
Kerchneia, good to drink, and Lerna's spring.
The earth-born herdsman Argos followed me
whose anger knew no limits, and he spied   680
after my tracks with all his hundred eyes.
Then an unlooked-for doom, descending suddenly,
took him from life: I, driven by the gadfly,
that god-sent scourge, was driven always onward
from one land to another: that is my story.
If you can tell me what remains for me,
tell me, and do not out of pity cozen
with kindly lies: there is no sickness worse
for me than words that to be kind must lie.

Chorus
    Hold! Keep away! Alas!
    never did I think that such strange

words would come to my ears:
never did I think such intolerable   690
sufferings, an offense to the eye,
shameful and frightening, so
would chill my soul with a double-edged point.
Alas, Alas, for your fate!
I shudder when I look on Io's fortune.

Prometheus

You groan too soon: you are full of fear too soon: wait till you
hear besides what is to be.

Chorus

Speak, tell us to the end. For sufferers it is sweet to know before-
hand clearly the pain that still remains for them.

Prometheus

The first request you made of me you gained   700
lightly: from her you wished to hear the story
of what she suffered. Now hear what remains,
what sufferings this maid must yet endure
from Hera. Do you listen, child of Inachus,
hear and lay up my words within your heart
that you may know the limits of your journey.
First turn to the sun's rising and walk on
over the fields no plough has broken: then
you will come to the wandering Scythians
who live in wicker houses built above
their well-wheeled wagons; they are an armed people,   710
armed with the bow that strikes from far away:
do not draw near them; rather let your feet
touch the surf line of the sea where the waves moan,
and cross their country: on your left there live
the Chalybes who work with iron: these
you must beware of; for they are not gentle,
nor people whom a stranger dare approach.
Then you will come to Insolence, a river
that well deserves its name: but cross it not—

it is no stream that you can easily ford—
until you come to Caucasus itself,
the highest mountains, where the river's strength   720
gushes from its very temples. Cross these peaks,
the neighbors of the stars, and take the road
southward until you reach the Amazons,
the race of women who hate men, who one day
shall live around Thermodon in Themiscyra
where Salmydessos, rocky jaw of the sea,
stands sailor-hating, stepmother of ships.
The Amazons will set you on your way
and gladly: you will reach Cimmeria,
the isthmus, at the narrow gates of the lake.   730
Leave this with a good heart and cross the channel,
the channel of Maeotis: and hereafter
for all time men shall talk about your crossing,
and they shall call the place for you Cow's-ford.*
Leave Europe's mainland then, and go to Asia.

(*To the Chorus*)

Do you now think this tyrant of the Gods
is hard in all things without difference?
He was a God and sought to lie in love
with this girl who was mortal, and on her
he brought this curse of wandering: bitter indeed
you found your marriage with this suitor, maid.
Yet you must think of all that I have told you
as still only in prelude.   740

Io

O, O

Prometheus

Again, you are crying and lamenting: what will you do when you
hear of the evils to come?

* Cow's-ford: Bosporus.

Chorus

Is there still something else to her sufferings of which you will speak?

Prometheus

A wintry sea of agony and ruin.

Io

What good is life to me then? Why do I not throw myself at once from some rough crag, to strike the ground and win a quittance of all my troubles? It would be better to die once for all than suffer all one's days. · 750

Prometheus

You would ill bear my trials, then, for whom Fate reserves no death. Death would be a quittance of trouble: but for me there is no limit of suffering set till Zeus fall from power.

Io

Can Zeus ever fall from power?

Prometheus

You would be glad to see that catastrophe, I think.

Io

Surely, since Zeus is my persecutor.

Prometheus

Then know that this shall be. 760

Io

Who will despoil him of his sovereign scepter?

Prometheus

His own witless plans.

Io

How? Tell me, if there is no harm to telling.

Prometheus

He shall make a marriage that shall hurt him.

Io

With god or mortal? Tell me, if you may say it.

Prometheus

Why ask what marriage? That is not to be spoken.

Io

Is it his wife shall cast him from his throne?

Prometheus

She shall bear him a son mightier than his father.

Io

Has he no possibility of escaping this downfall?

Prometheus

None, save through my release from these chains.   770

Io

But who will free you, against Zeus's will?

Prometheus

Fate has determined that it be one of your descendants.

Io

What, shall a child of mine bring you free?

Prometheus

Yes, in the thirteenth generation.

Io

Your prophecy has now passed the limits of understanding.

Prometheus

Then also do not seek to learn your trials.

Io

Do not offer me a boon and then withhold it.

Prometheus

I offer you then one of two stories.

Io

Which? Tell me and give me the choice.

Prometheus

I will: choose that I tell you clearly either what remains for you   780
or the one that shall deliver me.

Chorus

Grant her one and grant me the other and do not deny us the tale.
Tell her what remains of her wanderings: tell us of the one that
shall deliver you. That is what I desire.

Prometheus

    Since you have so much eagerness, I will not
    refuse to tell you all that you have asked me.
    First to you, Io, I shall tell the tale
    of your sad wanderings, rich in groans—inscribe
    the story in the tablets of your mind.   790
    When you shall cross the channel that divides
    Europe from Asia, turn to the rising sun,
    to the burnt plains, sun-scorched; cross by the edge
    of the foaming sea till you come to Gorgona
    to the flat stretches of Kisthene's country.
    There live the ancient maids, children of Phorcys:
    these swan-formed hags, with but one common eye,
    single-toothed monsters, such as nowhere else
    the sun's rays look on nor the moon by night.
    Near are their winged sisters, the three Gorgons,
    with snakes to bind their hair up, mortal-hating: 800
    nor mortal that but looks on them shall live:
    these are the sentry guards I tell you of.
    Hear, too, of yet another gruesome sight,
    the sharp-toothed hounds of Zeus, that have no bark,
    the vultures—them take heed of—and the host
    of one-eyed Arimaspians, horse-riding,
    that live around the spring which flows with gold,
    the spring of Pluto's river: go not near them.
    A land far off, a nation of black men,
    these you shall come to, men who live hard by
    the fountain of the sun where is the river
    Aethiops—travel by his banks along   810
    to a waterfall where from the Bibline hills
    Nile pours his holy waters, pure to drink.
    This river shall be your guide to the triangular
    land of the Nile and there, by Fate's decree,
    there, Io, you shall find your distant home,
    a colony for you and your descendants.

If anything of this is still obscure
or difficult ask me again and learn
clearly: I have more leisure than I wish.

Chorus

If there is still something left for you to tell her of her ruinous
wanderings, tell it; but if you have said everything, grant us the   820
favor we asked and tell us the story too.

Prometheus

The limit of her wanderings complete
she now has heard: but so that she may know
that she has not been listening to no purpose
I shall recount what she endured before
she came to us here: this I give as pledge,
a witness to the good faith of my words.
The great part of the story I omit
and come to the very boundary of your travels.
When you had come to the Molossian plains
around the sheer back of Dodona where   830
is the oracular seat of Zeus Thesprotian,
the talking oaks, a wonder past belief,
by them full clearly, in no riddling terms,
you were hailed glorious wife of Zeus that shall be:
does anything of this wake pleasant memories?
Then, goaded by the gadfly, on you hastened
to the great gulf of Rhea by the track
at the side of the sea: but in returning course
you were storm-driven back: in time to come
that inlet of the sea shall bear your name
and shall be called Ionian, a memorial   840
to all men of your journeying: these are proofs
for you, of how far my mind sees something farther
than what is visible: for what is left,
to you and you this I shall say in common,
taking up again the track of my old tale.
There is a city, furthest in the world,

Canobos, near the mouth and issuing point
of the Nile: there Zeus shall make you sound of mind
touching you with a hand that brings no fear,
and through that touch alone shall come your healing.   850
You shall bear Epaphos, dark of skin, his name
recalling Zeus's touch and his begetting.
This Epaphos shall reap the fruit of all
the land that is watered by the broad flowing Nile.
From him five generations, and again
to Argos they shall come, against their will,
in number fifty, women, flying from
a marriage with their kinsfolk: but these kinsfolk
their hearts with lust aflutter like the hawks
barely outdistanced by the doves will come
hunting a marriage that the law forbids:
the God shall grudge the men these women's bodies,
and the Pelasgian earth shall welcome them   860
in death: for death shall claim them in a fight
where women strike in the dark, a murderous vigil.
Each wife shall rob her husband of his life
dipping in blood her two-edged sword: even so
may Love come, too, upon my enemies.
But one among these girls shall love beguile
from killing her bedfellow, blunting her purpose:
and she shall make her choice—to bear the name
of coward and not murder: this girl,
she shall in Argos bear a race of kings.
To tell this clearly needs a longer story,   870
but from her seed shall spring a man renowned
for archery, and he shall set me free.
Such was the prophecy which ancient Themis
my Titan mother opened up to me;
but how and by what means it shall come true
would take too long to tell, and if you heard
the knowledge would not profit you.

Io

Eleleu, eleleu
It creeps on me again, the twitching spasm,
the mind-destroying madness, burning me up
and the gadfly's sting goads me on—
steel point by no fire tempered—
and my heart in its fear knocks on my breast.
There's a dazing whirl in my eyes as I run
out of my course by the madness driven,
the crazy frenzy; my tongue ungoverned
babbles, the words in a muddy flow strike
on the waves of the mischief I hate, strike wild
without aim or sense.

880

Chorus

STROPHE

A wise man indeed he was
that first in judgment weighed this word
and gave it tongue: the best by far
it is to marry in one's rank and station:
let no one working with her hands aspire
to marriage with those lifted high in pride
because of wealth, or of ancestral glory.

890

ANTISTROPHE

Never, never may you see me,
Fates majestic, drawing nigh
the bed of Zeus, to share it with the kings:
nor ever may I know a heavenly wooer:
I dread such things beholding
Io's sad virginity
ravaged, ruined; bitter wandering
hers because of Hera's wrath.

900

EPODE

When a match has equal partners
then I fear not: may the eye

inescapable of the mighty
Gods not look on me.
That is a fight that none can fight: a fruitful
source of fruitlessness: I would not
know what I could do: I cannot
see the hope when Zeus is angry
of escaping him.

Prometheus

Yet shall this Zeus, for all his pride of heart
be humble yet: such is the match he plans,
a marriage that shall drive him from his power
and from his throne, out of the sight of all.   910
So shall at last the final consummation
be brought about of Father Kronos' curse
which he, driven from his ancient throne, invoked
against the son deposing him: no one
of all the Gods save I alone can tell
a way to escape this mischief: I alone
know it and how. So let him confidently
sit on his throne and trust his heavenly thunder
and brandish in his hand his fiery bolt.
Nothing shall all of this avail against   920
a fall intolerable, a dishonored end.
So strong a wrestler Zeus is now equipping
against himself, a monster hard to fight.
This enemy shall find a plan to best
the thunderbolt, a thunderclap to best
the thunderclap of Zeus: and he shall shiver
Poseidon's trident, curse of sea and land.
So, in his crashing fall shall Zeus discover
how different are rule and slavery.

Chorus

You voice your wishes for the God's destruction.

Prometheus

They are my wishes, yet shall come to pass.

Chorus

Must we expect someone to conquer Zeus?   930

Prometheus

Yes; he shall suffer worse than I do now.

Chorus

Have you no fear of uttering such words?

Prometheus

Why should I fear, since death is not my fate?

Chorus

But he might give you pain still worse than this.

Prometheus

Then let him do so; all this I expect.

Chorus

Wise are the worshipers of Adrasteia

Prometheus

Worship him, pray; flatter whatever king
is king today; but I care less than nothing
for Zeus. Let him do what he likes,
let him be king for his short time: he shall not   940
be king for long.
             Look, here is Zeus's footman,
this fetch-and-carry messenger of him,
the New King. Certainly he has come here
with news for us.

Hermes

             You, subtle-spirit, you
bitterly overbitter, you that sinned
against the immortals, giving honor to
the creatures of a day, you thief of fire:
the Father has commanded you to say
what marriage of his is this you brag about
that shall drive him from power—and declare it   950

in clear terms and no riddles. You, Prometheus,
do not cause me a double journey; these

(*Pointing to the chains.*)

will prove to you that Zeus is not softhearted.

Prometheus

Your speech is pompous sounding, full of pride,
as fits the lackey of the Gods. You are young
and young your rule and you think that the tower
in which you live is free from sorrow: from it
have I not seen two tyrants thrown? the third,
who now is king, I shall yet live to see him
fall, of all three most suddenly, most dishonored.
Do you think I will crouch before your Gods,   960
—so new—and tremble? I am far from that.
Hasten away, back on the road you came.
You shall learn nothing that you ask of me.

Hermes

Just such the obstinacy that brought you here,
to this self-willed calamitous anchorage.

Prometheus

Be sure of this: when I set my misfortune
against your slavery, I would not change.

Hermes

It is better, I suppose, to be a slave
to this rock, than Zeus's trusted messenger.

Prometheus

Thus must the insolent show their insolence!   970

Hermes

I think you find your present lot too soft.

Prometheus

Too soft? I would my enemies had it then,
and you are one of those I count as such.

Hermes

Oh, you would blame me too for your calamity?

Prometheus
In a single word, I am the enemy
of all the Gods that gave me ill for good.

Hermes
Your words declare you mad, and mad indeed.

Prometheus
Yes, if it's madness to detest my foes.

Hermes
No one could bear you in success.

Prometheus
Alas!

Hermes
Alas! Zeus does not know that word.   980

Prometheus
Time in its aging course teaches all things.

Hermes
But you have not yet learned a wise discretion.

Prometheus
True: or I would not speak so to a servant.

Hermes
It seems you will not grant the Father's wish.

Prometheus
I should be glad, indeed, to requite his kindness!

Hermes
You mock me like a child!

Prometheus
And are you not
a child, and sillier than a child, to think
that I should tell you anything? There is not
a torture or an engine wherewithal
Zeus can induce me to declare these things,   990
till he has loosed me from these cruel shackles.
So let him hurl his smoky lightning flame,

and throw in turmoil all things in the world
with white-winged snowflakes and deep bellowing
thunder beneath the earth: me he shall not
bend by all this to tell him who is fated
to drive him from his tyranny.

Hermes

Think, here and now, if this seems to your interest.

Prometheus

I have already thought—and laid my plans.

Hermes

Bring your proud heart to know a true discretion—
O foolish spirit—in the face of ruin.   1000

Prometheus

You vex me by these senseless adjurations,
senseless as if you were to advise the waves.
Let it not cross your mind that I will turn
womanish-minded from my fixed decision
or that I shall entreat the one I hate
so greatly, with a woman's upturned hands,
to loose me from my chains: I am far from that.

Hermes

I have said too much already—so I think—
and said it to no purpose: you are not softened:
your purpose is not dented by my prayers.
You are a colt new broken, with the bit   1010
clenched in its teeth, fighting against the reins,
and bolting. You are far too strong and confident
in your weak cleverness. For obstinacy
standing alone is the weakest of all things
in one whose mind is not possessed by wisdom.
Think what a storm, a triple wave of ruin
will rise against you, if you will not hear me,
and no escape for you. First this rough crag
with thunder and the lightning bolt the Father

shall cleave asunder, and shall hide your body
wrapped in a rocky clasp within its depth;
a tedious length of time you must fulfil   1020
before you see the light again, returning.
Then Zeus's winged hound, the eagle red,
shall tear great shreds of flesh from you, a feaster
coming unbidden, every day: your liver
bloodied to blackness will be his repast.
And of this pain do not expect an end
until some God shall show himself successor
to take your tortures for himself and willing
go down to lightless Hades and the shadows
of Tartarus' depths. Bear this in mind
and so determine. This is no feigned boast   1030
but spoken with too much truth. The mouth of Zeus
does not know how to lie, but every word
brings to fulfilment. Look, you, and reflect
and never think that obstinacy is better
than prudent counsel.

Chorus
                          Hermes seems to us
to speak not altogether out of season.
He bids you leave your obstinacy and seek
a wise good counsel. Hearken to him. Shame
it were for one so wise to fall in error.

Prometheus
Before he told it me I knew this message: 1040
but there is no disgrace in suffering
at an enemy's hand, when you hate mutually.
So let the curling tendril of the fire
from the lightning bolt be sent against me: let
the air be stirred with thunderclaps, the winds
in savage blasts convulsing all the world.
Let earth to her foundations shake, yes to her root,
before the quivering storm: let it confuse

the paths of heavenly stars and the sea's waves
in a wild surging torrent: this my body
let Him raise up on high and dash it down   1050
into black Tartarus with rigorous
compulsive eddies: death he cannot give me.

Hermes

These are a madman's words, a madman's plan:
is there a missing note in this mad harmony?
is there a slack chord in his madness? You,
you, who are so sympathetic with his troubles,
away with you from here, quickly away!   1060
lest you should find your wits stunned by the thunder
and its hard defending roar.

Chorus

                          Say something else
different from this: give me some other counsel
that I will listen to: this word of yours
for all its instancy is not for us.
How dare you bid us practice baseness? We
will bear along with him what we must bear.
I have learned to hate all traitors: there is no
disease I spit on more than treachery.   1070

Hermes

Remember then my warning before the act:
when you are trapped by ruin don't blame fortune:
don't say that Zeus has brought you to calamity
that you could not foresee: do not do this:
but blame yourselves: now you know what you're doing:
and with this knowledge neither suddenly
nor secretly your own want of good sense
has tangled you in the net of ruin, past
all hope of rescue.

Prometheus
Now it is words no longer: now in very truth   1080
the earth is staggered: in its depths the thunder
bellows resoundingly, the fiery tendrils
of the lightning flash light up, and whirling clouds
carry the dust along: all the winds' blasts
dance in a fury one against the other
in violent confusion: earth and sea
are one, confused together: such is the storm
that comes against me manifestly from Zeus
to work its terrors. O Holy mother mine,   1090
O Sky that circling brings the light to all,
you see me, how I suffer, how unjustly.

OEDIPUS THE KING

Translated by David Grene

INTRODUCTION

The date is unknown. Most scholars are inclined to place it about 427 B.C., after the great plague at Athens, which is thought to have suggested the plague at Thebes in the play. But there is no reliable evidence. We happen to be told that this play, on its first presentation, gained only the second prize.

Aeschylus had already composed a Theban trilogy, of which an *Oedipus* (lost) was the second play, and we may assume that the largest outlines of the story were familiar to all. Or at least so much: that it was predicted that Oedipus would kill his father and marry his mother; that, unwittingly, he did both; and that these offenses were discovered and made public. Concerning details, there were certainly variations. There were different stories about how and where Oedipus died; Euripides in his lost *Oedipus* had the hero blinded by the henchmen of Laius; the traditions about Antigone and Ismene are not fixed.

Still, in *Oedipus the King*, once the hero appears and announces his identity, the audience will know the great glaring facts about Oedipus and will realize almost at once that Oedipus does not know these facts. The situation makes for a story heavily charged with irony. The advance of the action consists of a probing into the past. Every "act" or episode brings in a new "helper"—Oedipus himself, Creon, Teiresias, Jocasta, Messenger, Herdsman—each of whom contributes his clue, until the whole secret is out. A fresh dimension of irony lies in the fact that the ghastly tragedy is mounted on the frame of a happy romance—the lost baby miraculously saved, thought dead but restored and *united with his parents*. The search for the murderer of Laius and the identity of Oedipus come out at the same point. The discovery is the climax.

It would be difficult to interpret *Oedipus the King* as a story of the punishment of pride. The deeds for which the hero would be "punished" were preordained before he was even conceived. But it is true that the endowments which make him grand—his impulsive intellect, his passion for truth, his great physical strength, his integrity, and his pride—are all necessarily used to work out the pattern of his fate down to its final fulfilment in the realization of what that fate has been.

Even among the plays of Sophocles, *Oedipus the King* stands out for its poetry, the sinewy, intense composition of the spoken passages, and the wild splendor of the choral odes.

CHARACTERS

Oedipus, King of Thebes

Jocasta, His Wife

Creon, His Brother-in-Law

Teiresias, an Old Blind Prophet

A Priest

First Messenger

Second Messenger

A Herdsman

A Chorus of Old Men of Thebes

OEDIPUS THE KING

SCENE: *In front of the palace of Oedipus at Thebes. To the right of the stage near the altar stands the Priest with a crowd of children. Oedipus emerges from the central door.*

Oedipus

    Children, young sons and daughters of old Cadmus,
    why do you sit here with your suppliant crowns?
    The town is heavy with a mingled burden
    of sounds and smells, of groans and hymns and incense;   5
    I did not think it fit that I should hear
    of this from messengers but came myself,—
    I Oedipus whom all men call the Great.

                          (He turns to the Priest.)

    You're old and they are young; come, speak for them.
    What do you fear or want, that you sit here   10
    suppliant? Indeed I'm willing to give all
    that you may need; I would be very hard
    should I not pity suppliants like these.

Priest

    O ruler of my country, Oedipus,
    you see our company around the altar;   15
    you see our ages; some of us, like these,
    who cannot yet fly far, and some of us
    heavy with age; these children are the chosen
    among the young, and I the priest of Zeus.
    Within the market place sit others crowned   20
    with suppliant garlands, at the double shrine
    of Pallas and the temple where Ismenus
    gives oracles by fire. King, you yourself
    have seen our city reeling like a wreck
    already; it can scarcely lift its prow
    out of the depths, out of the bloody surf.

A blight is on the fruitful plants of the earth,   25
A blight is on the cattle in the fields,
a blight is on our women that no children
are born to them; a God that carries fire,
a deadly pestilence, is on our town,
strikes us and spares not, and the house of Cadmus
is emptied of its people while black Death
grows rich in groaning and in lamentation.   30
We have not come as suppliants to this altar
because we thought of you as of a God,
but rather judging you the first of men
in all the chances of this life and when
we mortals have to do with more than man.
You came and by your coming saved our city,   35
freed us from tribute which we paid of old
to the Sphinx, cruel singer. This you did
in virtue of no knowledge we could give you,
in virtue of no teaching; it was God
that aided you, men say, and you are held
with God's assistance to have saved our lives.
Now Oedipus, Greatest in all men's eyes,   40
here falling at your feet we all entreat you,
find us some strength for rescue.
Perhaps you'll hear a wise word from some God,
perhaps you will learn something from a man
(for I have seen that for the skilled of practice
the outcome of their counsels live the most).   45
Noblest of men, go, and raise up our city,
go,—and give heed. For now this land of ours
calls you its savior since you saved it once.
So, let us never speak about your reign
as of a time when first our feet were set
secure on high, but later fell to ruin.   50
Raise up our city, save it and raise it up.
Once you have brought us luck with happy omen;
be no less now in fortune.

If you will rule this land, as now you rule it,
better to rule it full of men than empty.   55
For neither tower nor ship is anything
when empty, and none live in it together.

Oedipus

I pity you, children. You have come full of longing,
but I have known the story before you told it
only too well. I know you are all sick,
yet there is not one of you, sick though you are,   60
that is as sick as I myself.
Your several sorrows each have single scope
and touch but one of you. My spirit groans
for city and myself and you at once.
You have not roused me like a man from sleep;   65
know that I have given many tears to this,
gone many ways wandering in thought,
but as I thought I found only one remedy
and that I took. I sent Menoeceus' son
Creon, Jocasta's brother, to Apollo,   70
to his Pythian temple,
that he might learn there by what act or word
I could save this city. As I count the days,
it vexes me what ails him; he is gone
far longer than he needed for the journey.   75
But when he comes, then, may I prove a villain,
if I shall not do all the God commands.

Priest

Thanks for your gracious words. Your servants here
signal that Creon is this moment coming.

Oedipus

His face is bright. O holy Lord Apollo,   80
grant that his news too may be bright for us
and bring us safety.

Priest

>It is happy news,
>I think, for else his head would not be crowned
>with sprigs of fruitful laurel.

Oedipus

>   We will know soon,
>he's within hail. Lord Creon, my good brother,   85
>what is the word you bring us from the God?

>   *(Creon enters.)*

Creon

>A good word,—for things hard to bear themselves
>if in the final issue all is well
>I count complete good fortune.

Oedipus

>   What do you mean?
>What you have said so far
>leaves me uncertain whether to trust or fear.   90

Creon

>If you will hear my news before these others
>I am ready to speak, or else to go within.

Oedipus

>Speak it to all;
>the grief I bear, I bear it more for these
>than for my own heart.

Creon

>   I will tell you, then,   95
>what I heard from the God.
>King Phoebus in plain words commanded us
>to drive out a pollution from our land,
>pollution grown ingrained within the land;
>drive it out, said the God, not cherish it,
>till it's past cure.

Oedipus

>   What is the rite
>of purification? How shall it be done?

Creon

> By banishing a man, or expiation   100
> of blood by blood, since it is murder guilt
> which holds our city in this destroying storm.

Oedipus

> Who is this man whose fate the God pronounces?

Creon

> My Lord, before you piloted the state
> we had a king called Laius.

Oedipus

> I know of him by hearsay. I have not seen him.   105

Creon

> The God commanded clearly: let some one
> punish with force this dead man's murderers.

Oedipus

> Where are they in the world? Where would a trace
> of this old crime be found? It would be hard
> to guess where.

Creon

>   The clue is in this land;   110
> that which is sought is found;
> the unheeded thing escapes:
> so said the God.

Oedipus

>   Was it at home,
> or in the country that death came upon him,
> or in another country travelling?

Creon

> He went, he said himself, upon an embassy,
> but never returned when he set out from home.   115

Oedipus

> Was there no messenger, no fellow traveller
> who knew what happened? Such a one might tell
> something of use.

Creon

They were all killed save one. He fled in terror
and he could tell us nothing in clear terms
of what he knew, nothing, but one thing only.

Oedipus

What was it?   120
If we could even find a slim beginning
in which to hope, we might discover much.

Creon

This man said that the robbers they encountered
were many and the hands that did the murder
were many; it was no man's single power.

Oedipus

How could a robber dare a deed like this
were he not helped with money from the city,
money and treachery?   125

Creon

                              That indeed was thought.
But Laius was dead and in our trouble
there was none to help.

Oedipus

What trouble was so great to hinder you
inquiring out the murder of your king?

Creon

The riddling Sphinx induced us to neglect   130
mysterious crimes and rather seek solution
of troubles at our feet.

Oedipus

I will bring this to light again. King Phoebus
fittingly took this care about the dead,
and you too fittingly.
And justly you will see in me an ally,   135
a champion of my country and the God.
For when I drive pollution from the land

I will not serve a distant friend's advantage,
but act in my own interest. Whoever
he was that killed the king may readily
wish to dispatch me with his murderous hand;   140
so helping the dead king I help myself.

Come, children, take your suppliant boughs and go;
up from the altars now. Call the assembly
and let it meet upon the understanding
that I'll do everything. God will decide   145
whether we prosper or remain in sorrow.

Priest
   Rise, children—it was this we came to seek,
   which of himself the king now offers us.
   May Phoebus who gave us the oracle
   come to our rescue and stay the plague.   150

                    (*Exeunt all but the Chorus.*)

Chorus
   Strophe
   What is the sweet spoken word of God from the shrine of Pytho
      rich in gold
   that has come to glorious Thebes?
   I am stretched on the rack of doubt, and terror and trembling
      hold
   my heart, O Delian Healer, and I worship full of fears
   for what doom you will bring to pass, new or renewed in the   155
      revolving years.
   Speak to me, immortal voice,
   child of golden Hope.

   Antistrophe
   First I call on you, Athene, deathless daughter of Zeus,
   and Artemis, Earth Upholder,   160
   who sits in the midst of the market place in the throne which
      men call Fame,
   and Phoebus, the Far Shooter, three averters of Fate,

come to us now, if ever before, when ruin rushed upon the state,   165
you drove destruction's flame away
out of our land.

Strophe
Our sorrows defy number;
all the ship's timbers are rotten;
taking of thought is no spear for the driving away of the plague.   170
There are no growing children in this famous land;
there are no women bearing the pangs of childbirth.
You may see them one with another, like birds swift on the
    wing,   175
quicker than fire unmastered,
speeding away to the coast of the Western God.

Antistrophe
In the unnumbered deaths
of its people the city dies;
those children that are born lie dead on the naked earth
unpitied, spreading contagion of death; and grey haired mothers
    and wives
everywhere stand at the altar's edge, suppliant, moaning;   182-85
the hymn to the healing God rings out but with it the wailing
    voices are blended.
From these our sufferings grant us, O golden Daughter of Zeus,
glad-faced deliverance.

Strophe
There is no clash of brazen shields but our fight is with the War
    God,
a War God ringed with the cries of men, a savage God who burns   191
    us;
grant that he turn in racing course backwards out of our coun-
    try's bounds
to the great palace of Amphitrite or where the waves of the   195
    Thracian sea
deny the stranger safe anchorage.
Whatsoever escapes the night

at last the light of day revisits;
so smite the War God, Father Zeus,
beneath your thunderbolt,
for you are the Lord of the lightning, the lightning that
    carries fire.   200

Antistrophe
And your unconquered arrow shafts, winged by the golden
    corded bow,
Lycean King, I beg to be at our side for help;   205
and the gleaming torches of Artemis with which she scours the
    Lycean hills,
and I call on the God with the turban of gold, who gave his name
    to this country of ours,   210
the Bacchic God with the wind flushed face,
Evian One, who travel
with the Maenad company,
combat the God that burns us
with your torch of pine;
for the God that is our enemy is a God unhonoured among the   215
    Gods.
                                       (Oedipus returns.)

Oedipus
For what you ask me—if you will hear my words,
and hearing welcome them and fight the plague,
you will find strength and lightening of your load.

Hark to me; what I say to you, I say
as one that is a stranger to the story
as stranger to the deed. For I would not   220
be far upon the track if I alone
were tracing it without a clue. But now,
since after all was finished, I became
a citizen among you, citizens—
now I proclaim to all the men of Thebes:
who so among you knows the murderer   225
by whose hand Laius, son of Labdacus,

died—I command him to tell everything
to me,—yes, though he fears himself to take the blame
on his own head; for bitter punishment
he shall have none, but leave this land unharmed.
Or if he knows the murderer, another,   230
a foreigner, still let him speak the truth.
For I will pay him and be grateful, too.
But if you shall keep silence, if perhaps
some one of you, to shield a guilty friend,
or for his own sake shall reject my words—
hear what I shall do then: 235
I forbid that man, whoever he be, my land,
my land where I hold sovereignty and throne;
and I forbid any to welcome him
or cry him greeting or make him a sharer   240
in sacrifice or offering to the Gods,
or give him water for his hands to wash.
I command all to drive him from their homes,
since he is our pollution, as the oracle
of Pytho's God proclaimed him now to me.
So I stand forth a champion of the God
and of the man who died.   245
Upon the murderer I invoke this curse—
whether he is one man and all unknown,
or one of many—may he wear out his life
in misery to miserable doom!
If with my knowledge he lives at my hearth   250
I pray that I myself may feel my curse.
On you I lay my charge to fulfill all this
for me, for the God, and for this land of ours
destroyed and blighted, by the God forsaken.

Even were this no matter of God's ordinance   255
it would not fit you so to leave it lie,
unpurified, since a good man is dead
and one that was a king. Search it out.

Since I am now the holder of his office,
and have his bed and wife that once was his,   260
and had his line not been unfortunate
we would have common children—(fortune leaped
upon his head)—because of all these things,
I fight in his defence as for my father,
and I shall try all means to take the murderer   265
of Laius the son of Labdacus
the son of Polydorus and before him
of Cadmus and before him of Agenor.
Those who do not obey me, may the Gods
grant no crops springing from the ground they plough   270
nor children to their women! May a fate
like this, or one still worse than this consume them!
For you whom these words please, the other Thebans,
may Justice as your ally and all the Gods
live with you, blessing you now and for ever!   275

Chorus

As you have held me to my oath, I speak:
I neither killed the king nor can declare
the killer; but since Phoebus set the quest
it is his part to tell who the man is.

Oedipus

Right; but to put compulsion on the Gods   280
against their will—no man can do that.

Chorus

May I then say what I think second best?

Oedipus

If there's a third best, too, spare not to tell it.

Chorus

I know that what the Lord Teiresias
sees, is most often what the Lord Apollo   285
sees. If you should inquire of this from him
you might find out most clearly.

Oedipus
    Even in this my actions have not been sluggard.
    On Creon's word I have sent two messengers
    and why the prophet is not here already
    I have been wondering.

Chorus
                    His skill apart   290
    there is besides only an old faint story.

Oedipus
    What is it?
    I look at every story.

Chorus
                  It was said
    that he was killed by certain wayfarers.

Oedipus
    I heard that, too, but no one saw the killer.

Chorus
    Yet if he has a share of fear at all,
    his courage will not stand firm, hearing your curse.   295

Oedipus
    The man who in the doing did not shrink
    will fear no word.

Chorus
             Here comes his prosecutor:
    led by your men the godly prophet comes
    in whom alone of mankind truth is native.

                  (Enter Teiresias, led by a little boy.)

Oedipus
    Teiresias, you are versed in everything,   300
    things teachable and things not to be spoken,
    things of the heaven and earth-creeping things.
    You have no eyes but in your mind you know
    with what a plague our city is afflicted.
    My lord, in you alone we find a champion,

in you alone one that can rescue us.
Perhaps you have not heard the messengers,   305
but Phoebus sent in answer to our sending
an oracle declaring that our freedom
from this disease would only come when we
should learn the names of those who killed King Laius,
and kill them or expel from our country.
Do not begrudge us oracles from birds,   310
or any other way of prophecy
within your skill; save yourself and the city,
save me; redeem the debt of our pollution
that lies on us because of this dead man.
We are in your hands; pains are most nobly taken
to help another when you have means and power.   315

Teiresias
Alas, how terrible is wisdom when
it brings no profit to the man that's wise!
This I knew well, but had forgotten it,
else I would not have come here.

Oedipus
                              What is this?
How sad you are now you have come!

Teiresias
                              Let me
go home. It will be easiest for us both   320
to bear our several destinies to the end
if you will follow my advice.

Oedipus
                         You'd rob us
of this your gift of prophecy? You talk
as one who had no care for law nor love
for Thebes who reared you.

Teiresias
Yes, but I see that even your own words
miss the mark; therefore I must fear for mine.   325

Oedipus

    For God's sake if you know of anything,
    do not turn from us; all of us kneel to you,
    all of us here, your suppliants.

Teiresias

    All of you here know nothing. I will not
    bring to the light of day my troubles, mine—
    rather than call them yours.

Oedipus

                What do you mean?
    You know of something but refuse to speak.   330
    Would you betray us and destroy the city?

Teiresias

    I will not bring this pain upon us both,
    neither on you nor on myself. Why is it
    you question me and waste your labour? I
    will tell you nothing.

Oedipus

    You would provoke a stone! Tell us, you villain,   335
    tell us, and do not stand there quietly
    unmoved and balking at the issue.

Teiresias

    You blame my temper but you do not see
    your own that lives within you; it is me
    you chide.

Oedipus

    Who would not feel his temper rise
    at words like these with which you shame our city?   340

Teiresias

    Of themselves things will come, although I hide them
    and breathe no word of them.

Oedipus

               Since they will come
    tell them to me.

Teiresias

I will say nothing further.
Against this answer let your temper rage
as wildly as you will.

Oedipus

Indeed I am   345
so angry I shall not hold back a jot
of what I think. For I would have you know
I think you were complotter of the deed
and doer of the deed save in so far
as for the actual killing. Had you had eyes
I would have said alone you murdered him.

Teiresias

Yes? Then I warn you faithfully to keep   350
the letter of your proclamation and
from this day forth to speak no word of greeting
to these nor me; you are the land's pollution.

Oedipus

How shamelessly you started up this taunt!
How do you think you will escape?   355

Teiresias

I have.
I have escaped; the truth is what I cherish
and that's my strength.

Oedipus

And who has taught you truth?
Not your profession surely!

Teiresias

You have taught me,
for you have made me speak against my will.

Oedipus

Speak what? Tell me again that I may learn it better.

Teiresias

Did you not understand before or would you
provoke me into speaking?   360

Oedipus

        I did not grasp it,
not so to call it known. Say it again.

Teiresias

 I say you are the murderer of the king
whose murderer you seek.

Oedipus

        Not twice you shall
say calumnies like this and stay unpunished.

Teiresias

 Shall I say more to tempt your anger more?

Oedipus

 As much as you desire; it will be said   365
in vain.

Teiresias

      I say that with those you love best
you live in foulest shame unconsciously
and do not see where you are in calamity.

Oedipus

 Do you imagine you can always talk
like this, and live to laugh at it hereafter?

Teiresias

 Yes, if the truth has anything of strength.

Oedipus

 It has, but not for you; it has no strength   370
for you because you are blind in mind and ears
as well as in your eyes.

Teiresias

      You are a poor wretch
to taunt me with the very insults which
every one soon will heap upon yourself.

Oedipus

 Your life is one long night so that you cannot
hurt me or any other who sees the light.   375

Teiresias
　It is not fate that I should be your ruin,
　Apollo is enough; it is his care
　to work this out.

Oedipus
　　　　　　　　　Was this your own design
　or Creon's?

Teiresias
　　　　　　　Creon is no hurt to you,
　but you are to yourself.

Oedipus
　Wealth, sovereignty and skill outmatching skill　　　380
　for the contrivance of an envied life!
　Great store of jealousy fill your treasury chests,
　if my friend Creon, friend from the first and loyal,　385
　thus secretly attacks me, secretly
　desires to drive me out and secretly
　suborns this juggling, trick devising quack,
　this wily beggar who has only eyes
　for his own gains, but blindness in his skill.
　For, tell me, where have you seen clear, Teiresias,　390
　with your prophetic eyes? When the dark singer,
　the sphinx, was in your country, did you speak
　word of deliverance to its citizens?
　And yet the riddle's answer was not the province
　of a chance comer. It was a prophet's task
　and plainly you had no such gift of prophecy　　　395
　from birds nor otherwise from any God
　to glean a word of knowledge. But I came,
　Oedipus, who knew nothing, and I stopped her.
　I solved the riddle by my wit alone.
　Mine was no knowledge got from birds. And now
　you would expel me,
　because you think that you will find a place　　　400
　by Creon's throne. I think you will be sorry,

both you and your accomplice, for your plot
to drive me out. And did I not regard you
as an old man, some suffering would have taught you
that what was in your heart was treason.

Chorus

We look at this man's words and yours, my king,
and we find both have spoken them in anger.   405
We need no angry words but only thought
how we may best hit the God's meaning for us.

Teiresias

If you are king, at least I have the right
no less to speak in my defence against you.
Of that much I am master. I am no slave   410
of yours, but Loxias', and so I shall not
enroll myself with Creon for my patron.
Since you have taunted me with being blind,
here is my word for you.
You have your eyes but see not where you are
in sin, nor where you live, nor whom you live with.
Do you know who your parents are? Unknowing   415
you are an enemy to kith and kin
in death, beneath the earth, and in this life.
A deadly footed, double striking curse,
from father and mother both, shall drive you forth
out of this land, with darkness on your eyes,
that now have such straight vision. Shall there be
a place will not be harbour to your cries,   420
a corner of Cithaeron will not ring
in echo to your cries, soon, soon,—
when you shall learn the secret of your marriage,
which steered you to a haven in this house,—
haven no haven, after lucky voyage?
And of the multitude of other evils
establishing a grim equality
between you and your children, you know nothing. 425

So, muddy with contempt my words and Creon's!
Misery shall grind no man as it will you.

Oedipus

Is it endurable that I should hear
such words from him? Go and a curse go with you!   430
Quick, home with you! Out of my house at once!

Teiresias

I would not have come either had you not called me.

Oedipus

I did not know then you would talk like a fool—
or it would have been long before I called you.

Teiresias

I am a fool then, as it seems to you—   435
but to the parents who have bred you, wise.

Oedipus

What parents? Stop! Who are they of all the world?

Teiresias

This day will show your birth and will destroy you.

Oedipus

How needlessly your riddles darken everything.

Teiresias

But it's in riddle answering you are strongest.   440

Oedipus

Yes. Taunt me where you will find me great.

Teiresias

It is this very luck that has destroyed you.

Oedipus

I do not care, if it has saved this city.

Teiresias

Well, I will go. Come, boy, lead me away.

Oedipus

Yes, lead him off. So long as you are here,   445

you'll be a stumbling block and a vexation;
once gone, you will not trouble me again.

Teiresias

                    I have said
what I came here to say not fearing your
countenance: there is no way you can hurt me.
I tell you, king, this man, this murderer
(whom you have long declared you are in search of,
indicting him in threatening proclamation   450
as murderer of Laius)—he is here.
In name he is a stranger among citizens
but soon he will be shown to be a citizen
true native Theban, and he'll have no joy
of the discovery: blindness for sight
and beggary for riches his exchange,   455
he shall go journeying to a foreign country
tapping his way before him with a stick.
He shall be proved father and brother both
to his own children in his house; to her
that gave him birth, a son and husband both;
a fellow sower in his father's bed
with that same father that he murdered.
Go within, reckon that out, and if you find me   460
mistaken, say I have no skill in prophecy.

                    (*Exeunt separately Teiresias and Oedipus.*)

Chorus

   Strophe
Who is the man proclaimed
by Delphi's prophetic rock
as the bloody handed murderer,   465
the doer of deeds that none dare name?
Now is the time for him to run
with a stronger foot
than Pegasus
for the child of Zeus leaps in arms upon him   470
with fire and the lightning bolt,

and terribly close on his heels
are the Fates that never miss.

Antistrophe
Lately from snowy Parnassus
clearly the voice flashed forth,
bidding each Theban track him down,   475
the unknown murderer.
In the savage forests he lurks and in
the caverns like
the mountain bull.
He is sad and lonely, and lonely his feet
that carry him far from the navel of earth;   480
but its prophecies, ever living,
flutter around his head.

Strophe
The augur has spread confusion,
terrible confusion;
I do not approve what was said   485
nor can I deny it.
I do not know what to say;
I am in a flutter of foreboding;
I never heard in the present
nor past of a quarrel between   490
the sons of Labdacus and Polybus,
that I might bring as proof
in attacking the popular fame
of Oedipus, seeking
to take vengeance for undiscovered
death in the line of Labdacus.   495

Antistrophe
Truly Zeus and Apollo are wise
and in human things all knowing;
but amongst men there is no   500
distinct judgment, between the prophet
and me—which of us is right.

One man may pass another in wisdom
but I would never agree
with those that find fault with the king
till I should see the word
proved right beyond doubt. For once
in visible form the Sphinx
came on him and all of us
saw his wisdom and in that test
he saved the city. So he will not be condemned by my mind.   512

(*Enter Creon.*)

Creon

Citizens, I have come because I heard
deadly words spread about me, that the king
accuses me. I cannot take that from him.
If he believes that in these present troubles   515
he has been wronged by me in word or deed
I do not want to live on with the burden
of such a scandal on me. The report   520
injures me doubly and most vitally—
for I'll be called a traitor to my city
and traitor also to my friends and you.

Chorus

Perhaps it was a sudden gust of anger
that forced that insult from him, and no judgment.

Creon

But did he say that it was in compliance   525
with schemes of mine that the seer told him lies?

Chorus

Yes, he said that, but why, I do not know.

Creon

Were his eyes straight in his head? Was his mind right
when he accused me in this fashion?

Chorus

I do not know; I have no eyes to see   530
what princes do. Here comes the king himself.

(Enter Oedipus.)

Oedipus

    You, sir, how is it you come here? Have you so much
    brazen-faced daring that you venture in
    my house although you are proved manifestly
    the murderer of that man, and though you tried,
    openly, highway robbery of my crown? 535
    For God's sake, tell me what you saw in me,
    what cowardice or what stupidity,
    that made you lay a plot like this against me?
    Did you imagine I should not observe
    the crafty scheme that stole upon me or
    seeing it, take no means to counter it? 540
    Was it not stupid of you to make the attempt,
    to try to hunt down royal power without
    the people at your back or friends? For only
    with the people at your back or money can
    the hunt end in the capture of a crown.

Creon

    Do you know what you're doing? Will you listen
    to words to answer yours, and then pass judgment?

Oedipus

    You're quick to speak, but I am slow to grasp you, 545
    for I have found you dangerous,—and my foe.

Creon

    First of all hear what I shall say to that.

Oedipus

    At least don't tell me that you are not guilty.

Creon

    If you think obstinacy without wisdom
    a valuable possession, you are wrong. 550

Oedipus

    And you are wrong if you believe that one,
    a criminal, will not be punished only
    because he is my kinsman.

Creon

This is but just—
but tell me, then, of what offense I'm guilty?

Oedipus

Did you or did you not urge me to send   555
to this prophetic mumbler?

Creon

I did indeed,
and I shall stand by what I told you.

Oedipus

How long ago is it since Laius. . . .

Creon

What about Laius? I don't understand.

Oedipus

Vanished—died—was murdered?   560

Creon

It is long,
a long, long time to reckon.

Oedipus

Was this prophet
in the profession then?

Creon

He was, and honoured
as highly as he is today.

Oedipus

At that time did he say a word about me?

Creon

Never, at least when I was near him.   565

Oedipus

You never made a search for the dead man?

Creon

We searched, indeed, but never learned of anything.

Oedipus

Why did our wise old friend not say this then?

Creon
I don't know; and when I know nothing, I
usually hold my tongue.

Oedipus
                    You know this much,   570
and can declare this much if you are loyal.

Creon
What is it? If I know, I'll not deny it.

Oedipus
That he would not have said that I killed Laius
had he not met you first.

Creon
                    You know yourself
whether he said this, but I demand that I   575
should hear as much from you as you from me.

Oedipus
Then hear,—I'll not be proved a murderer.

Creon
Well, then. You're married to my sister.

Oedipus
                    Yes,
that I am not disposed to deny.

Creon
                    You rule
this country giving her an equal share
in the government?

Oedipus
                    Yes, everything she wants   580
she has from me.

Creon
                    And I, as thirdsman to you,
am rated as the equal of you two?

Oedipus
Yes, and it's there you've proved yourself false friend.

Creon

Not if you will reflect on it as I do.
Consider, first, if you think any one
would choose to rule and fear rather than rule   585
and sleep untroubled by a fear if power
were equal in both cases. I, at least,
I was not born with such a frantic yearning
to be a king—but to do what kings do.
And so it is with every one who has learned
wisdom and self-control. As it stands now,
the prizes are all mine—and without fear.   590
But if I were the king myself, I must
do much that went against the grain.
How should despotic rule seem sweeter to me
than painless power and an assured authority?
I am not so besotted yet that I
want other honours than those that come with profit.   595
Now every man's my pleasure; every man greets me;
now those who are your suitors fawn on me,—
success for them depends upon my favour.
Why should I let all this go to win that?
My mind would not be traitor if it's wise;   600
I am no treason lover, of my nature,
nor would I ever dare to join a plot.
Prove what I say. Go to the oracle
at Pytho and inquire about the answers,
if they are as I told you. For the rest,   605
if you discover I laid any plot
together with the seer, kill me, I say,
not only by your vote but by my own.
But do not charge me on obscure opinion
without some proof to back it. It's not just
lightly to count your knaves as honest men,   610
nor honest men as knaves. To throw away
an honest friend is, as it were, to throw
your life away, which a man loves the best.

In time you will know all with certainty;
time is the only test of honest men,
one day is space enough to know a rogue.   615

Chorus

His words are wise, king, if one fears to fall.
Those who are quick of temper are not safe.

Oedipus

When he that plots against me secretly
moves quickly, I must quickly counterplot.
If I wait taking no decisive measure   620
his business will be done, and mine be spoiled.

Creon

What do you want to do then? Banish me?

Oedipus

No, certainly; kill you, not banish you.'

Creon

I do not think that you've your wits about you.   626

Oedipus

For my own interests, yes.

Creon

But for mine, too,
you should think equally.

Oedipus

You are a rogue.

Creon

Suppose you do not understand?

Oedipus

But yet
I must be ruler.

1. Two lines omitted here owing to the confusion in the dialogue consequent on
the loss of a third line. The lines as they stand in Jebb's edition (1902) are:
Oed.: That you may show what manner of thing is envy.
Creon: You speak as one that will not yield or trust.
[Oed. lost line.]

Creon

Not if you rule badly.

Oedipus

O, city, city!

Creon

I too have some share   630
in the city; it is not yours alone.

Chorus

Stop, my lords! Here—and in the nick of time
I see Jocasta coming from the house;
with her help lay the quarrel that now stirs you.

(*Enter Jocasta.*)

Jocasta

For shame! Why have you raised this foolish squabbling
brawl? Are you not ashamed to air your private   630
griefs when the country's sick? Go in, you, Oedipus,
and you, too, Creon, into the house. Don't magnify
your nothing troubles.

Creon

Sister, Oedipus,
your husband, thinks he has the right to do
terrible wrongs—he has but to choose between   640
two terrors: banishing or killing me.

Oedipus

He's right, Jocasta; for I find him plotting
with knavish tricks against my person.

Creon

That God may never bless me! May I die
accursed, if I have been guilty of   645
one tittle of the charge you bring against me!

Jocasta

I beg you, Oedipus, trust him in this,
spare him for the sake of this his oath to God,
for my sake, and the sake of those who stand here.

Chorus

Be gracious, be merciful,   649
we beg of you.

Oedipus

In what would you have me yield?

Chorus

He has been no silly child in the past.
He is strong in his oath now.
Spare him.

Oedipus

Do you know what you ask?

Chorus

Yes.

Oedipus

Tell me then.

Chorus

He has been your friend before all men's eyes; do not cast him   656
away dishonoured on an obscure conjecture.

Oedipus

I would have you know that this request of yours
really requests my death or banishment.

Chorus

May the Sun God, king of Gods, forbid! May I die without God's   660
blessing, without friends' help, if I had any such thought. But my
spirit is broken by my unhappiness for my wasting country; and   665
this would but add troubles amongst ourselves to the other
troubles.

Oedipus

Well, let him go then—if I must die ten times for it,   669
or be sent out dishonoured into exile.
It is your lips that prayed for him I pitied,
not his; wherever he is, I shall hate him.

Creon

    I see you sulk in yielding and you're dangerous
    when you are out of temper; natures like yours
    are justly heaviest for themselves to bear.   675

Oedipus

    Leave me alone! Take yourself off, I tell you.

Creon

    I'll go, you have not known me, but they have,
    and they have known my innocence.

                                                   (*Exit.*)

Chorus

    Won't you take him inside, lady?

Jocasta

    Yes, when I've found out what was the matter.   680

Chorus

    There was some misconceived suspicion of a story, and on the
    other side the sting of injustice.

Jocasta

    So, on both sides?

Chorus

    Yes.

Jocasta

    What was the story?

Chorus

    I think it best, in the interests of the country, to leave it where   685
    it ended.

Oedipus

    You see where you have ended, straight of judgment
    although you are, by softening my anger.

Chorus

    Sir, I have said before and I say again—be sure that I would have   689
    been proved a madman, bankrupt in sane council, if I should put
    you away, you who steered the country I love safely when she

was crazed with troubles. God grant that now, too, you may   695
prove a fortunate guide for us.

Jocasta

Tell me, my lord, I beg of you, what was it
that roused your anger so?

Oedipus

Yes, I will tell you.   700
I honour you more than I honour them.
It was Creon and the plots he laid against me.

Jocasta

Tell me—if you can clearly tell the quarrel—

Oedipus

Creon says
that I'm the murderer of Laius.

Jocasta

Of his own knowledge or on information?

Oedipus

He sent this rascal prophet to me, since   705
he keeps his own mouth clean of any guilt.

Jocasta

Do not concern yourself about this matter;
listen to me and learn that human beings
have no part in the craft of prophecy.
Of that I'll show you a short proof.   710
There was an oracle once that came to Laius,—
I will not say that it was Phoebus' own,
but it was from his servants—and it told him
that it was fate that he should die a victim
at the hands of his own son, a son to be born
of Laius and me. But, see now, he,
the king, was killed by foreign highway robbers   715
at a place where three roads meet—so goes the story;
and for the son—before three days were out
after his birth King Laius pierced his ankles

and by the hands of others cast him forth
upon a pathless hillside. So Apollo   720
failed to fulfill his oracle to the son,
that he should kill his father, and to Laius
also proved false in that the thing he feared,
death at his son's hands, never came to pass.
So clear in this case were the oracles,
so clear and false. Give them no heed, I say;
what God discovers need of, easily
he shows to us himself.   725

Oedipus

                O dear Jocasta,
as I hear this from you, there comes upon me
a wandering of the soul—I could run mad.

Jocasta

What trouble is it, that you turn again
and speak like this?

Oedipus

                I thought I heard you say
that Laius was killed at a crossroads.   730

Jocasta

Yes, that was how the story went and still
that word goes round.

Oedipus

              Where is this place, Jocasta,
where he was murdered?

Jocasta

             Phocis is the country
and the road splits there, one of two roads from Delphi,
another comes from Daulia.

Oedipus

             How long ago is this?   735

Jocasta

The news came to the city just before

you became king and all men's eyes looked to you.
What is it, Oedipus, that's in your mind?

Oedipus
What have you designed, O Zeus, to do with me?

Jocasta
What is the thought that troubles your heart?

Oedipus
Don't ask me yet—tell me of Laius—   740
How did he look? How old or young was he?

Jocasta
He was a tall man and his hair was grizzled
already—nearly white—and in his form
not unlike you.

Oedipus
                              O God, I think I have
called curses on myself in ignorance.   745

Jocasta
What do you mean? I am terrified
when I look at you.

Oedipus
                              I have a deadly fear
that the old seer had eyes. You'll show me more
if you can tell me one more thing.

Jocasta
                                          I will.
I'm frightened,—but if I can understand,
I'll tell you all you ask.

Oedipus
                              How was his company?   750
Had he few with him when he went this journey,
or many servants, as would suit a prince?

Jocasta
In all there were but five, and among them
a herald; and one carriage for the king.

Oedipus

It's plain—its plain—who was it told you this?   755

Jocasta

The only servant that escaped safe home.

Oedipus

Is he at home now?

Jocasta

                    No, when he came home again
and saw you king and Laius was dead,
he came to me and touched my hand and begged   760
that I should send him to the fields to be
my shepherd and so he might see the city
as far off as he might. So I
sent him away. He was an honest man,
as slaves go, and was worthy of far more
than what he asked of me.

Oedipus

O, how I wish that he could come back quickly!   765

Jocasta

He can. Why is your heart so set on this?

Oedipus

O dear Jocasta, I am full of fears
that I have spoken far too much; and therefore
I wish to see this shepherd.

Jocasta

                   He will come;
but, Oedipus, I think I'm worthy too
to know what it is that disquiets you.   770

Oedipus

It shall not be kept from you, since my mind
has gone so far with its forebodings. Whom
should I confide in rather than you, who is there
of more importance to me who have passed
through such a fortune?

Polybus was my father, king of Corinth,
and Merope, the Dorian, my mother.   775
I was held greatest of the citizens
in Corinth till a curious chance befell me
as I shall tell you—curious, indeed,
but hardly worth the store I set upon it.
There was a dinner and at it a man,
a drunken man, accused me in his drink   780
of being bastard. I was furious
but held my temper under for that day.
Next day I went and taxed my parents with it;
they took the insult very ill from him,
the drunken fellow who had uttered it.
So I was comforted for their part, but   785
still this thing rankled always, for the story
crept about widely. And I went at last
to Pytho, though my parents did not know.
But Phoebus sent me home again unhonoured
in what I came to learn, but he foretold   790
other and desperate horrors to befall me,
that I was fated to lie with my mother,
and show to daylight an accursed breed
which men would not endure, and I was doomed
to be murderer of the father that begot me.
When I heard this I fled, and in the days
that followed I would measure from the stars   795
the whereabouts of Corinth—yes, I fled
to somewhere where I should not see fulfilled
the infamies told in that dreadful oracle.
And as I journeyed I came to the place
where, as you say, this king met with his death.
Jocasta, I will tell you the whole truth.   800
When I was near the branching of the crossroads,
going on foot, I was encountered by
a herald and a carriage with a man in it,
just as you tell me. He that led the way

and the old man himself wanted to thrust me   805
out of the road by force. I became angry
and struck the coachman who was pushing me.
When the old man saw this he watched his moment,
and as I passed he struck me from his carriage,
full on the head with his two pointed goad.
But he was paid in full and presently   810
my stick had struck him backwards from the car
and he rolled out of it. And then I killed them
all. If it happened there was any tie
of kinship twixt this man and Laius,
who is then now more miserable than I,   815
what man on earth so hated by the Gods,
since neither citizen nor foreigner
may welcome me at home or even greet me,
but drive me out of doors? And it is I,
I and no other have so cursed myself.   820
And I pollute the bed of him I killed
by the hands that killed him. Was I not born evil?
Am I not utterly unclean? I had to fly
and in my banishment not even see
my kindred nor set foot in my own country,
or otherwise my fate was to be yoked   825
in marriage with my mother and kill my father,
Polybus who begot me and had reared me.
Would not one rightly judge and say that on me
these things were sent by some malignant God?
O no, no, no—O holy majesty   830
of God on high, may I not see that day!
May I be gone out of men's sight before
I see the deadly taint of this disaster
come upon me.

Chorus

Sir, we too fear these things. But until you see this man face to
face and hear his story, hope.   835

Oedipus

Yes, I have just this much of hope—to wait until the herdsman comes.

Jocasta

And when he comes, what do you want with him?

Oedipus

I'll tell you; if I find that his story is the same as yours, I at least will be clear of this guilt. 840

Jocasta

Why what so particularly did you learn from my story?

Oedipus

You said that he spoke of highway *robbers* who killed Laius. Now if he uses the same number, it was not I who killed him. One man cannot be the same as many. But if he speaks of a man travelling 845 alone, then clearly the burden of the guilt inclines towards me.

Jocasta

Be sure, at least, that this was how he told the story. He cannot unsay it now, for every one in the city heard it—not I alone. But, 850 Oedipus, even if he diverges from what he said then, he shall never prove that the murder of Laius squares rightly with the prophecy—for Loxias declared that the king should be killed by his own son. And that poor creature did not kill him surely,— 855 for he died himself first. So as far as prophecy goes, henceforward I shall not look to the right hand or the left.

Oedipus

Right. But yet, send some one for the peasant to bring him here; 860 do not neglect it.

Jocasta

I will send quickly. Now let me go indoors. I will do nothing except what pleases you.

(*Exeunt.*)

Chorus

  Strophe

May destiny ever find me

pious in word and deed   865
prescribed by the laws that live on high:
laws begotten in the clear air of heaven,
whose only father is Olympus;
no mortal nature brought them to birth,
no forgetfulness shall lull them to sleep;   870
for God is great in them and grows not old.

Antistrophe

Insolence breeds the tyrant, insolence
if it is glutted with a surfeit, unseasonable, unprofitable,   875
climbs to the roof-top and plunges
sheer down to the ruin that must be,
and there its feet are no service.
But I pray that the God may never   880
abolish the eager ambition that profits the state.
For I shall never cease to hold the God as our protector.

Strophe

If a man walks with haughtiness
of hand or word and gives no heed   885
to Justice and the shrines of Gods
despises—may an evil doom
smite him for his ill-starred pride of heart!—
if he reaps gains without justice
and will not hold from impiety   890
and his fingers itch for untouchable things.
When such things are done, what man shall contrive
to shield his soul from the shafts of the God?
When such deeds are held in honour,   895
why should I honour the Gods in the dance?

Antistrophe

No longer to the holy place,
to the navel of earth I'll go
to worship, nor to Abae
nor to Olympia,   900
unless the oracles are proved to fit,
for all men's hands to point at.

O Zeus, if you are rightly called
the sovereign lord, all-mastering,
let this not escape you nor your ever-living power!   905
The oracles concerning Laius
are old and dim and men regard them not.
Apollo is nowhere clear in honour; God's service perishes.   910

(Enter Jocasta, carrying garlands.)

Jocasta
Princes of the land, I have had the thought to go
to the Gods' temples, bringing in my hand
garlands and gifts of incense, as you see.
For Oedipus excites himself too much
at every sort of trouble, not conjecturing,   915
like a man of sense, what will be from what was,
but he is always at the speaker's mercy,
when he speaks terrors. I can do no good
by my advice, and so I came as suppliant
to you, Lycaean Apollo, who are nearest.
These are the symbols of my prayer and this   920
my prayer: grant us escape free of the curse.
Now when we look to him we are all afraid;
he's pilot of our ship and he is frightened.

(Enter Messenger.)

Messenger
Might I learn from you, sirs, where is the house of Oedipus? Or   925
best of all, if you know, where is the king himself?

Chorus
This is his house and he is within doors. This lady is his wife and
mother of his children.

Messenger
God bless you, lady, and God bless your household! God bless   930
Oedipus' noble wife!

Jocasta
God bless you, sir, for your kind greeting! What do you want
of us that you have come here? What have you to tell us?

Messenger

Good news, lady. Good for your house and for your husband.

Jocasta

What is your news? Who sent you to us? 935

Messenger

I come from Corinth and the news I bring will give you pleasure. Perhaps a little pain too.

Jocasta

What is this news of double meaning?

Messenger

The people of the Isthmus will choose Oedipus to be their king. 940
That is the rumour there.

Jocasta

But isn't their king still old Polybus?

Messenger

No. He is in his grave. Death has got him.

Jocasta

Is that the truth? Is Oedipus' father dead?

Messenger

May I die myself if it be otherwise!

Jocasta (to a servant)

Be quick and run to the King with the news! O oracles of the 945
Gods, where are you now? It was from this man Oedipus fled, lest
he should be his murderer! And now he is dead, in the course of
nature, and not killed by Oedipus.

(*Enter Oedipus.*)

Oedipus

Dearest Jocasta, why have you sent for me? 950

Jocasta

Listen to this man and when you hear reflect what is the outcome
of the holy oracles of the Gods.

Oedipus

Who is he? What is his message for me?

Jocasta

    He is from Corinth and he tells us that your father Polybus is   955
dead and gone.

Oedipus

    What's this you say, sir? Tell me yourself.

Messenger

    Since this is the first matter you want clearly told: Polybus has
gone down to death. You may be sure of it.

Oedipus

    By treachery or sickness?   960

Messenger

    A small thing will put old bodies asleep.

Oedipus

    So he died of sickness, it seems,—poor old man!

Messenger

    Yes, and of age—the long years he had measured.

Oedipus

    Ha! Ha! O dear Jocasta, why should one
look to the Pythian hearth? Why should one look   965
to the birds screaming overhead? They prophesied
that I should kill my father! But he's dead,
and hidden deep in earth, and I stand here
who never laid a hand on spear against him,—
unless perhaps he died of longing for me,
and thus I am his murderer. But they,   970
the oracles, as they stand—he's taken them
away with him, they're dead as he himself is,
and worthless.

Jocasta

                  That I told you before now.

Oedipus

    You did, but I was misled by my fear.

Jocasta

    Then lay no more of them to heart, not one   975

Oedipus

But surely I must fear my mother's bed?

Jocasta

Why should man fear since chance is all in all
for him, and he can clearly foreknow nothing?
Best to live lightly, as one can, unthinkingly.
As to your mother's marriage bed,—don't fear it.   980
Before this, in dreams too, as well as oracles,
many a man has lain with his own mother.
But he to whom such things are nothing bears
his life most easily.

Oedipus

All that you say would be said perfectly
if she were dead; but since she lives I must   985
still fear, although you talk so well, Jocasta.

Jocasta

Still in your father's death there's light of comfort?

Oedipus

Great light of comfort; but I fear the living.

Messenger

Who is the woman that makes you afraid?

Oedipus

Merope, old man, Polybus' wife.   990

Messenger

What about her frightens the queen and you?

Oedipus

A terrible oracle, stranger, from the Gods.

Messenger

Can it be told? Or does the sacred law
forbid another to have knowledge of it?

Oedipus

O no! Once on a time Loxias said
that I should lie with my own mother and   995

take on my hands the blood of my own father.
And so for these long years I've lived away
from Corinth; it has been to my great happiness;
but yet it's sweet to see the face of parents.

Messenger
This was the fear which drove you out of Corinth?   1000

Oedipus
Old man, I did not wish to kill my father.

Messenger
Why should I not free you from this fear, sir,
since I have come to you in all goodwill?

Oedipus
You would not find me thankless if you did.

Messenger
Why, it was just for this I brought the news,—   1005
to earn your thanks when you had come safe home.

Oedipus
No, I will never come near my parents.

Messenger
                                            Son,
it's very plain you don't know what you're doing.

Oedipus
What do you mean, old man? For God's sake, tell me.

Messenger
If your homecoming is checked by fears like these.   1010

Oedipus
Yes, I'm afraid that Phoebus may prove right.

Messenger
The murder and the incest?

Oedipus
                                        Yes, old man;
that is my constant terror.

Messenger

Do you know
that all your fears are empty?

Oedipus

How is that,   1015
if they are father and mother and I their son?

Messenger

Because Polybus was no kin to you in blood.

Oedipus

What, was not Polybus my father?

Messenger

No more than I but just so much.

Oedipus

How can
my father be my father as much as one
that's nothing to me?

Messenger

Neither he nor I   1020
begat you.

Oedipus

Why then did he call me son?

Messenger

A gift he took you from these hands of mine.

Oedipus

Did he love so much what he took from another's hand?

Messenger

His childlessness before persuaded him.

Oedipus

Was I a child you bought or found when I   1025
was given to him?

Messenger

On Cithaeron's slopes
in the twisting thickets you were found.

Oedipus

                    And why
were you a traveller in those parts?

Messenger

                        I was
in charge of mountain flocks.

Oedipus

                    You were a shepherd?
A hireling vagrant?

Messenger

                        Yes, but at least at that time   1030
the man that saved your life, son.

Oedipus

What ailed me when you took me in your arms?

Messenger

In that your ankles should be witnesses.

Oedipus

Why do you speak of that old pain?

Messenger

                    I loosed you;
the tendons of your feet were pierced and fettered,—

Oedipus

My swaddling clothes brought me a rare disgrace.   1035

Messenger

So that from this you're called your present name.

Oedipus

Was this my father's doing or my mother's?
For God's sake, tell me.

Messenger

                    I don't know, but he
who gave you to me has more knowledge than I.

Oedipus

You yourself did not find me then? You took me
from someone else?

Messenger

                             Yes, from another shepherd.   1040

Oedipus

Who was he? Do you know him well enough
to tell?

Messenger

                             He was called Laius' man.

Oedipus

You mean the king who reigned here in the old days?

Messenger

Yes, he was that man's shepherd.

Oedipus

                          Is he alive   1045
still, so that I could see him?

Messenger

                         You who live here
would know that best.

Oedipus

                       Do any of you here
know of this shepherd whom he speaks about
in town or in the fields? Tell me. It's time   1050
that this was found out once for all.

Chorus

I think he is none other than the peasant
whom you have sought to see already; but
Jocasta here can tell us best of that.

Oedipus

Jocasta, do you know about this man
whom we have sent for? Is he the man he mentions?   1055

Jocasta

Why ask of whom he spoke? Don't give it heed;
nor try to keep in mind what has been said.
It will be wasted labour.

Oedipus
>   With such clues
> I could not fail to bring my birth to light.

Jocasta
> I beg you—do not hunt this out—I beg you,   1060
> if you have any care for your own life.
> What I am suffering is enough.

Oedipus
>   Keep up
> your heart, Jocasta. Though I'm proved a slave,
> thrice slave, and though my mother is thrice slave,
> you'll not be shown to be of lowly lineage.

Jocasta
> O be persuaded by me, I entreat you;
> do not do this.

Oedipus
> I will not be persuaded to let be   1065
> the chance of finding out the whole thing clearly.

Jocasta
> It is because I wish you well that I
> give you this counsel—and it's the best counsel.

Oedipus
> Then the best counsel vexes me, and has
> for some while since.

Jocasta
>   O Oedipus, God help you!
> God keep you from the knowledge of who you are!

Oedipus
> Here, some one, go and fetch the shepherd for me;
> and let her find her joy in her rich family!   1070

Jocasta
> O Oedipus, unhappy Oedipus!
> that is all I can call you, and the last thing
> that I shall ever call you.

>   (*Exit.*)

Chorus

Why has the queen gone, Oedipus, in wild
grief rushing from us? I am afraid that trouble   1075
will break out of this silence.

Oedipus

Break out what will! I at least shall be
willing to see my ancestry, though humble.
Perhaps she is ashamed of my low birth,
for she has all a woman's high-flown pride.
But I account myself a child of Fortune,   1080
beneficent Fortune, and I shall not be
dishonoured. She's the mother from whom I spring;
the months, my brothers, marked me, now as small,
and now again as mighty. Such is my breeding,
and I shall never prove so false to it,   1085
as not to find the secret of my birth.

Chorus

　Strophe

If I am a prophet and wise of heart
you shall not fail, Cithaeron,   1090
by the limitless sky, you shall not!—
to know at tomorrow's full moon
that Oedipus honours you,
as native to him and mother and nurse at once;
and that you are honoured in dancing by us, as finding favour in
　　sight of our king.
Apollo, to whom we cry, find these things pleasing!

　Antistrophe

Who was it bore you, child? One of   1098
the long-lived nymphs who lay with Pan—
the father who treads the hills?
Or was she a bride of Loxias, your mother? The grassy slopes
are all of them dear to him. Or perhaps Cyllene's king   1104
or the Bacchants' God that lives on the tops

of the hills received you a gift from some
one of the Helicon Nymphs, with whom he mostly plays?

(Enter an old man, led by Oedipus' servants.)

Oedipus

If some one like myself who never met him   1110
may make a guess,—I think this is the herdsman,
whom we were seeking. His old age is consonant
with the other. And besides, the men who bring him
I recognize as my own servants. You   1115
perhaps may better me in knowledge since
you've seen the man before.

Chorus
                You can be sure
I recognize him. For if Laius
had ever an honest shepherd, this was he.

Oedipus

You, sir, from Corinth, I must ask you first,
is this the man you spoke of?   1120

Messenger
             This is he
before your eyes.

Oedipus
           Old man, look here at me
and tell me what I ask you. Were you ever
a servant of King Laius?

Herdsman
           I was,—
no slave he bought but reared in his own house.

Oedipus

What did you do as work? How did you live?

Herdsman

Most of my life was spent among the flocks.   1125

Oedipus

In what part of the country did you live?

Herdsman

Cithaeron and the places near to it.

Oedipus

And somewhere there perhaps you knew this man?

Herdsman

What was his occupation? Who?

Oedipus

                This man here,   1130
have you had any dealings with him?

Herdsman

             No—
not such that I can quickly call to mind.

Messenger

That is no wonder, master. But I'll make him remember what he
does not know. For I know, that he well knows the country of
Cithaeron, how he with two flocks, I with one kept company for   1135
three years—each year half a year—from spring till autumn time
and then when winter came I drove my flocks to our fold home
again and he to Laius' steadings. Well—am I right or not in what   1140
I said we did?

Herdsman

You're right—although it's a long time ago.

Messenger

Do you remember giving me a child
to bring up as my foster child?

Herdsman

                What's this?
Why do you ask this question?

Messenger

               Look old man,   1145
here he is—here's the man who was that child!

Herdsman

Death take you! Won't you hold your tongue?

Oedipus

No, no,
do not find fault with him, old man. Your words
are more at fault than his.

Herdsman

O best of masters,
how do I give offense?

Oedipus

When you refuse   1150
to speak about the child of whom he asks you.

Herdsman

He speaks out of his ignorance, without meaning.

Oedipus

If you'll not talk to gratify me, you
will talk with pain to urge you.

Herdsman

O please, sir,
don't hurt an old man, sir.

Oedipus (to the servants)

Here, one of you,
twist his hands behind him.

Herdsman

Why, God help me, why?   1155
What do you want to know?

Oedipus

You gave a child
to him,—the child he asked you of?

Herdsman

I did.
I wish I'd died the day I did.

Oedipus

You will
unless you tell me truly.

Herdsman

And I'll die
far worse if I should tell you.

Oedipus

This fellow   1160
is bent on more delays, as it would seem.

Herdsman

O no, no! I have told you that I gave it.

Oedipus

Where did you get this child from? Was it your own or did you
get it from another?

Herdsman

Not
my own at all; I had it from some one.

Oedipus

One of these citizens? or from what house?

Herdsman

O master, please—I beg you, master, please   1165
don't ask me more.

Oedipus

You're a dead man if I
ask you again.

Herdsman

It was one of the children
of Laius.

Oedipus

A slave? Or born in wedlock?

Herdsman

O God, I am on the brink of frightful speech.

Oedipus

And I of frightful hearing. But I must hear.   1170

Herdsman

The child was called his child; but she within,
your wife would tell you best how all this was.

Oedipus
   She gave it to you?

Herdsman
                         Yes, she did, my lord.

Oedipus
   To do what with it?

Herdsman
                         Make away with it.

Oedipus
   She was so hard—its mother?   1175

Herdsman
                         Aye, through fear
   of evil oracles.

Oedipus
                         Which?

Herdsman
                         They said that he
   should kill his parents.

Oedipus
                         How was it that you
   gave it away to this old man?

Herdsman
                         O master,
   I pitied it, and thought that I could send it
   off to another country and this man
   was from another country. But he saved it   1180
   for the most terrible troubles. If you are
   the man he says you are, you're bred to misery.

Oedipus
   O, O, O, they will all come,
   all come out clearly! Light of the sun, let me
   look upon you no more after today!
   I who first saw the light bred of a match
   accursed, and accursed in my living
   with them I lived with, cursed in my killing.   1185

                         (*Exeunt all but the Chorus.*)

Chorus

    Strophe

O generations of men, how I
count you as equal with those who live
not at all!
What man, what man on earth wins more   1190
of happiness than a seeming
and after that turning away?
Oedipus, you are my pattern of this,
Oedipus, you and your fate!
Luckless Oedipus, whom of all men
I envy not at all.   1196

    Antistrophe

In as much as he shot his bolt
beyond the others and won the prize
of happiness complete—
O Zeus—and killed and reduced to nought
the hooked taloned maid of the riddling speech,
standing a tower against death for my land:
hence he was called my king and hence
was honoured the highest of all
honours; and hence he ruled
in the great city of Thebes.

    Strophe

But now whose tale is more miserable?   1204
Who is there lives with a savager fate?
Whose troubles so reverse his life as his?

O Oedipus, the famous prince
for whom a great haven
the same both as father and son
sufficed for generation,
how, O how, have the furrows ploughed
by your father endured to bear you, poor wretch,
and hold their peace so long?

Antistrophe
Time who sees all has found you out   1213
against your will; judges your marriage accursed,
begetter and begot at one in it.

O child of Laius,
would I had never seen you.
I weep for you and cry
a dirge of lamentation.

To speak directly, I drew my breath
from you at the first and so now I lull   1222
my mouth to sleep with your name.

                                 (*Enter a second messenger.*)

Second Messenger
O Princes always honoured by our country,
what deeds you'll hear of and what horrors see,
what grief you'll feel, if you as true born Thebans   1225
care for the house of Labdacus's sons.
Phasis nor Ister cannot purge this house,
I think, with all their streams, such things
it hides, such evils shortly will bring forth
into the light, whether they will or not;   1230
and troubles hurt the most
when they prove self-inflicted.

Chorus
What we had known before did not fall short
of bitter groaning's worth; what's more to tell?

Second Messenger
Shortest to hear and tell—our glorious queen   1235
Jocasta's dead.

Chorus
                      Unhappy woman! How?
Second Messenger
By her own hand. The worst of what was done
you cannot know. You did not see the sight.
Yet in so far as I remember it

you'll hear the end of our unlucky queen.   1240
When she came raging into the house she went
straight to her marriage bed, tearing her hair
with both her hands, and crying upon Laius   1245
long dead—Do you remember, Laius,
that night long past which bred a child for us
to send you to your death and leave
a mother making children with her son?
And then she groaned and cursed the bed in which
she brought forth husband by her husband, children   1250
by her own child, an infamous double bond.
How after that she died I do not know,—
for Oedipus distracted us from seeing.
He burst upon us shouting and we looked
to him as he paced frantically around,
begging us always: Give me a sword, I say,   1255
to find this wife no wife, this mother's womb,
this field of double sowing whence I sprang
and where I sowed my children! As he raved
some god showed him the way—none of us there.
Bellowing terribly and led by some   1260
invisible guide he rushed on the two doors,—
wrenching the hollow bolts out of their sockets,
he charged inside. There, there, we saw his wife
hanging, the twisted rope around her neck.
When he saw her, he cried out fearfully   1265
and cut the dangling noose. Then, as she lay,
poor woman, on the ground, what happened after,
was terrible to see. He tore the brooches—
the gold chased brooches fastening her robe—
away from her and lifting them up high
dashed them on his own eyeballs, shrieking out   1270
such things as: they will never see the crime
I have committed or had done upon me!
Dark eyes, now in the days to come look on
forbidden faces, do not recognize

those whom you long for—with such imprecations
he struck his eyes again and yet again   1275
with the brooches. And the bleeding eyeballs gushed
and stained his beard—no sluggish oozing drops
but a black rain and bloody hail poured down.

So it has broken—and not on one head   1280
but troubles mixed for husband and for wife.
The fortune of the days gone by was true
good fortune—but today groans and destruction
and death and shame—of all ills can be named   1285
not one is missing.

Chorus
Is he now in any ease from pain?

Second Messenger
                              He shouts
for some one to unbar the doors and show him
to all the men of Thebes, his father's killer,
his mother's—no I cannot say the word,
it is unholy—for he'll cast himself,
out of the land, he says, and not remain   1290
to bring a curse upon his house, the curse
he called upon it in his proclamation. But
he wants for strength, aye, and some one to guide him;
his sickness is too great to bear. You, too,
will be shown that. The bolts are opening.   1295
Soon you will see a sight to waken pity
even in the horror of it.
                              (*Enter the blinded Oedipus.*)

Chorus
This is a terrible sight for men to see!
I never found a worse!
Poor wretch, what madness came upon you!   1300
What evil spirit leaped upon your life
to your ill-luck—a leap beyond man's strength!
Indeed I pity you, but I cannot

look at you, though there's much I want to ask
and much to learn and much to see.   1305
I shudder at the sight of you.

Oedipus

O, O,
where am I going? Where is my voice   1310
borne on the wind to and fro?
Spirit, how far have you sprung?

Chorus

To a terrible place whereof men's ears
may not hear, nor their eyes behold it.

Oedipus

Darkness!
Horror of darkness enfolding, resistless, unspeakable visitant sped
    by an ill wind in haste!   1315
madness and stabbing pain and memory
of evil deeds I have done!

Chorus

In such misfortunes it's no wonder
if double weighs the burden of your grief.   1320

Oedipus

My friend,
you are the only one steadfast, the only one that attends on me;
you still stay nursing the blind man.
Your care is not unnoticed. I can know   1325
your voice, although this darkness is my world.

Chorus

Doer of dreadful deeds, how did you dare
so far to do despite to your own eyes?
what spirit urged you to it?

Oedipus

It was Apollo, friends, Apollo,
that brought this bitter bitterness, my sorrows to completion.   1330
But the hand that struck me

was none but my own.
Why should I see
whose vision showed me nothing sweet to see?   1335

Chorus
These things are as you say.

Oedipus
What can I see to love?
What greeting can touch my ears with joy?
Take me away, and haste—to a place out of the way!   1340
Take me away, my friends, the greatly miserable,
the most accursed, whom God too hates   1345
above all men on earth!

Chorus
Unhappy in your mind and your misfortune,
would I had never known you!

Oedipus
Curse on the man who took
the cruel bonds from off my legs, as I lay in the field.   1350
He stole me from death and saved me,
no kindly service.
Had I died then
I would not be so burdensome to friends.   1355

Chorus
I, too, could have wished it had been so.

Oedipus
Then I would not have come
to kill my father and marry my mother infamously.
Now I am godless and child of impurity,   1360
begetter in the same seed that created my wretched self.
If there is any ill worse than ill,   1365
that is the lot of Oedipus.

Chorus
I cannot say your remedy was good;
you would be better dead than blind and living.

Oedipus

What I have done here was best done—don't tell me   1370
otherwise, do not give me further counsel.
I do not know with what eyes I could look
upon my father when I die and go
under the earth, nor yet my wretched mother—
those two to whom I have done things deserving
worse punishment than hanging. Would the sight   1375
of children, bred as mine are, gladden me?
No, not these eyes, never. And my city,
its towers and sacred places of the Gods,
of these I robbed my miserable self   1380
when I commanded all to drive *him* out,
the criminal since proved by God impure
and of the race of Laius.
To this guilt I bore witness against myself—
with what eyes shall I look upon my people?   1385
No. If there were a means to choke the fountain
of hearing I would not have stayed my hand
from locking up my miserable carcase,
seeing and hearing nothing; it is sweet   1390
to keep our thoughts out of the range of hurt.

Cithaeron, why did you receive me? why
having received me did you not kill me straight?
And so I had not shown to men my birth.

O Polybus and Corinth and the house,
the old house that I used to call my father's—   1395
what fairness you were nurse to, and what foulness
festered beneath! Now I am found to be
a sinner and a son of sinners. Crossroads,
and hidden glade, oak and the narrow way
at the crossroads, that drank my father's blood   1400
offered you by my hands, do you remember
still what I did as you looked on, and what
I did when I came here? O marriage, marriage!

you bred me and again when you had bred
bred children of your child and showed to men   1405
brides, wives and mothers and the foulest deeds
that can be in this world of ours.

Come—it's unfit to say what is unfit
to do.—I beg of you in God's name hide me   1410
somewhere outside your country, yes, or kill me,
or throw me into the sea, to be forever
out of your sight. Approach and deign to touch me
for all my wretchedness, and do not fear.
No man but I can bear my evil doom.   1415

Chorus

Here Creon comes in fit time to perform
or give advice in what you ask of us.
Creon is left sole ruler in your stead.

Oedipus

Creon! Creon! What shall I say to him?
How can I justly hope that he will trust me?   1420
In what is past I have been proved towards him
an utter liar.

                            (Enter Creon.)

Creon

                  Oedipus, I've come
not so that I might laugh at you nor taunt you
with evil of the past. But if you still
are without shame before the face of men
reverence at least the flame that gives all life,   1425
our Lord the Sun, and do not show unveiled
to him pollution such that neither land
nor holy rain nor light of day can welcome.

                            (To a servant.)

Be quick and take him in. It is most decent   1430
that only kin should see and hear the troubles
of kin.

Oedipus
>   I beg you, since you've torn me from
my dreadful expectations and have come
in a most noble spirit to a man
that has used you vilely—do a thing for me.
I shall speak for your own good, not for my own.

Creon
What do you need that you would ask of me?   1435

Oedipus
Drive me from here with all the speed you can
to where I may not hear a human voice.

Creon
Be sure, I would have done this had not I
wished first of all to learn from the God the course
of action I should follow.

Oedipus
>   But his word   1440
has been quite clear to let the parricide,
the sinner, die.

Creon
>   Yes, that indeed was said.
But in the present need we had best discover
what we should do.

Oedipus
>   And will you ask about
a man so wretched?

Creon
>   Now even you will trust   1445
the God.

Oedipus
>   So. I command you—and will beseech you—
to her that lies inside that house give burial
as you would have it; she is yours and rightly
you will perform the rites for her. For me—

never let this my father's city have me   1450
living a dweller in it. Leave me live
in the mountains where Cithaeron is, that's called
my mountain, which my mother and my father
while they were living would have made my tomb.
So I may die by their decree who sought
indeed to kill me. Yet I know this much: 1455
no sickness and no other thing will kill me.
I would not have been saved from death if not
for some strange evil fate. Well, let my fate
go where it will.

      Creon, you need not care   1460
about my sons; they're men and so wherever
they are, they will not lack a livelihood.
But my two girls—so sad and pitiful—
whose table never stood apart from mine,
and everything I touched they always shared—   1465
O Creon, have a thought for them! And most
I wish that you might suffer me to touch them
and sorrow with them.

   (*Enter Antigone and Ismene, Oedipus' two daughters.*)
O my lord! O true noble Creon! Can I   1470
really be touching them, as when I saw?
What shall I say?
Yes, I can hear them sobbing—my two darlings!
and Creon has had pity and has sent me
what I loved most?
Am I right?   1475

Creon

 You're right: it was I gave you this
because I knew from old days how you loved them
as I see now.

Oedipus

     God bless you for it, Creon,
and may God guard you better on your road
than he did me!

O children, 1480

where are you? Come here, come to my hands,
a brother's hands which turned your father's eyes,
those bright eyes you knew once, to what you see,
a father seeing nothing, knowing nothing,
begetting you from his own source of life. 1485
I weep for you—I cannot see your faces—
I weep when I think of the bitterness
there will be in your lives, how you must live
before the world. At what assemblages
of citizens will you make one? to what 1490
gay company will you go and not come home
in tears instead of sharing in the holiday?
And when you're ripe for marriage, who will he be,
the man who'll risk to take such infamy
as shall cling to my children, to bring hurt 1495
on them and those that marry with them? What
curse is not there? "Your father killed his father
and sowed the seed where he had sprung himself
and begot you out of the womb that held him."
These insults you will hear. Then who will marry you? 1500
No one, my children; clearly you are doomed
to waste away in barrenness unmarried.
Son of Menoeceus, since you are all the father
left these two girls, and we, their parents, both 1505
are dead to them—do not allow them wander
like beggars, poor and husbandless.
They are of your own blood.
And do not make them equal with myself
in wretchedness; for you can see them now
so young, so utterly alone, save for you only.
Touch my hand, noble Creon, and say yes. 1510
If you were older, children, and were wiser,
there's much advice I'd give you. But as it is,
let this be what you pray: give me a life

wherever there is opportunity
to live, and better life than was my father's.

Creon
Your tears have had enough of scope; now go within the house.   1515

Oedipus
I must obey, though bitter of heart.

Creon
In season, all is good.

Oedipus
Do you know on what conditions I obey?

Creon
                              You tell me them,
and I shall know them when I hear.

Oedipus
                              That you shall send me out
to live away from Thebes.

Creon
                    That gift you must ask of the God.

Oedipus
But I'm now hated by the Gods.

Creon
                    So quickly you'll obtain your prayer.

Oedipus
You consent then?   1520

Creon
                    What I do not mean, I do not use to say.

Oedipus
Now lead me away from here.

Creon
                    Let go the children, then, and come.

Oedipus
Do not take them from me.

Creon

> Do not seek to be master in everything,
> for the things you mastered did not follow you throughout your
>   life.

> (*As Creon and Oedipus go out.*)

Chorus

> You that live in my ancestral Thebes, behold this Oedipus,—
> him who knew the famous riddles and was a man most masterful;   1525
> not a citizen who did not look with envy on his lot—
> see him now and see the breakers of misfortune swallow him!
> Look upon that last day always. Count no mortal happy till
> he has passed the final limit of his life secure from pain.   1530

ANTIGONE

Translated by Elizabeth Wyckoff

INTRODUCTION

Antigone was probably produced in 442 B.C. Though the part of the saga of Thebes with which it deals is subsequent to the action of *Oedipus the King*, and also *Oedipus at Colonus*, the drama itself was certainly the earliest written of the three, which therefore do not compose a formal trilogy.

We do not know how much of the story as told by Sophocles was already known to the audience which first saw the play. No foreknowledge is required. The contrast with *Oedipus the King* is striking. Here is no revelation of events that have already happened; instead, from an established situation, we drive straight ahead, through an unrelenting series of encounters, to the final catastrophe. No other Greek play is so fast off the mark. Yet the tragic irony is here as well, through the shape of the developing action, in the fact that Creon, acting always in the belief that he is sacrificing himself for the good of the community, gives way, but too late to save Antigone, Haemon, and Eurydice, who need not have died at all; and in the fact that Antigone dies thinking that Haemon has deserted her, when in fact he was faithful.

Through the conflicts between individuals who always remain sharply characterized is written the eternal conflict between private conscience and public authority. The magnificent choral odes carry the terms of this conflict into images which hold good for any time or place.

CHARACTERS

Antigone

Ismene

Chorus of Theban Elders

Creon

A Guard

Haemon

Teiresias

A Messenger

Eurydice

ANTIGONE

SCENE: *Thebes, before the royal palace. Antigone and Ismene emerge from its great central door.*

Antigone

My sister, my Ismene, do you know
of any suffering from our father sprung
that Zeus does not achieve for us survivors?
There's nothing grievous, nothing free from doom,
not shameful, not dishonored, I've not seen.
Your sufferings and mine.
And now, what of this edict which they say
the commander has proclaimed to the whole people?
Have you heard anything? Or don't you know
that the foes' trouble comes upon our friends?   10

Ismene

I've heard no word, Antigone, of our friends.
Not sweet nor bitter, since that single moment
when we two lost two brothers
who died on one day by a double blow.
And since the Argive army went away
this very night, I have no further news
of fortune or disaster for myself.

Antigone

I knew it well, and brought you from the house
for just this reason, that you alone may hear.

Ismene

What is it? Clearly some news has clouded you.   20

Antigone

It has indeed. Creon will give the one
of our two brothers honor in the tomb;
the other none.

Eteocles, with just entreatment treated,
as law provides he has hidden under earth
to have full honor with the dead below.
But Polyneices' corpse who died in pain,
they say he has proclaimed to the whole town
that none may bury him and none bewail,
but leave him unwept, untombed, a rich sweet sight
for the hungry birds' beholding.   30
Such orders they say the worthy Creon gives
to you and me—yes, yes, I say to *me*—
and that he's coming to proclaim it clear
to those who know it not.
Further: he has the matter so at heart
that anyone who dares attempt the act
will die by public stoning in the town.
So there you have it and you soon will show
if you are noble, or fallen from your descent.

Ismene
If things have reached this stage, what can I do,
poor sister, that will help to make or mend?   40

Antigone
Think will you share my labor and my act.

Ismene
What will you risk? And where is your intent?

Antigone
Will you take up that corpse along with me?

Ismene
To bury him you mean, when it's forbidden?

Antigone
My brother, and yours, though you may wish he were not.
I never shall be found to be his traitor.

Ismene
O hard of mind! When Creon spoke against it!

Antigone

It's not for him to keep me from my own.

Ismene

Alas. Remember, sister, how our father
perished abhorred, ill-famed.   50
Himself with his own hand, through his own curse
destroyed both eyes.
Remember next his mother and his wife
finishing life in the shame of the twisted strings.
And third two brothers on a single day,
poor creatures, murdering, a common doom
each with his arm accomplished on the other.
And now look at the two of us alone.
We'll perish terribly if we force law
and try to cross the royal vote and power.   60
We must remember that we two are women
so not to fight with men.
And that since we are subject to strong power
we must hear these orders, or any that may be worse.
So I shall ask of them beneath the earth
forgiveness, for in these things I am forced,
and shall obey the men in power. I know
that wild and futile action makes no sense.

Antigone

I wouldn't urge it. And if now you wished
to act, you wouldn't please me as a partner.   70
Be what you want to; but that man shall I
bury. For me, the doer, death is best.
Friend shall I lie with him, yes friend with friend,
when I have dared the crime of piety.
Longer the time in which to please the dead
than that for those up here.
There shall I lie forever. You may see fit
to keep from honor what the gods have honored.

Ismene

> I shall do no dishonor. But to act
> against the citizens. I cannot.

Antigone

> That's your protection. Now I go, to pile   80
> the burial-mound for him, my dearest brother.

Ismene

> Oh my poor sister. How I fear for you!

Antigone

> For me, don't borrow trouble. Clear your fate.

Ismene

> At least give no one warning of this act;
> you keep it hidden, and I'll do the same.

Antigone

> Dear God! Denounce me. I shall hate you more
> if silent, not proclaiming this to all.

Ismene

> You have a hot mind over chilly things.

Antigone

> I know I please those whom I most should please.

Ismene

> If but you can. You crave what can't be done.   90

Antigone

> And so, when strength runs out, I shall give over.

Ismene

> Wrong from the start, to chase what cannot be.

Antigone

> If that's your saying, I shall hate you first,
> and next the dead will hate you in all justice.
> But let me and my own ill-counselling
> suffer this terror. I shall suffer nothing
> as great as dying with a lack of grace.

Ismene

Go, since you want to. But know this: you go
senseless indeed, but loved by those who love you.

> (*Ismene returns to the palace; Antigone leaves by one of the side
> entrances. The Chorus now enters from the other side.*)

Chorus

Sun's own radiance, fairest light ever shone on the gates of
    Thebes,   100
then did you shine, O golden day's
eye, coming over Dirce's stream,
on the Man who had come from Argos with all his armor
running now in headlong fear as you shook his bridle free.

He was stirred by the dubious quarrel of Polyneices.   110
    So, screaming shrill,
    like an eagle over the land he flew,
    covered with white-snow wing,
    with many weapons,
    with horse-hair crested helms.

He who had stood above our halls, gaping about our seven gates,
with that circle of thirsting spears.
Gone, without our blood in his jaws,   120
before the torch took hold on our tower-crown.
Rattle of war at his back; hard the fight for the dragon's foe.

    The boasts of a proud tongue are for Zeus to hate.
    So seeing them streaming on
    in insolent clangor of gold,   130
    he struck with hurling fire him who rushed
    for the high wall's top,
    to cry conquest abroad.

Swinging, striking the earth he fell
fire in hand, who in mad attack,
had raged against us with blasts of hate.
He failed. He failed of his aim.

For the rest great Ares dealt his blows about,
first in the war-team.   140

    The captains stationed at seven gates
fought with seven and left behind
their brazen arms as an offering
to Zeus who is turner of battle.
All but those wretches, sons of one man,
one mother's sons, who sent their spears
each against each and found the share
of a common death together.

Great-named Victory comes to us
answering Thebe's warrior-joy.
Let us forget the wars just done   150
and visit the shrines of the gods.
All, with night-long dance which Bacchus will lead,
who shakes Thebe's acres.

                             (Creon enters from the palace.)

    Now here he comes, the king of the land,
Creon, Menoeceus' son,
newly named by the gods' new fate.
What plan that beats about his mind
has made him call this council-session,   160
sending his summons to all?

Creon

My friends, the very gods who shook the state
with mighty surge have set it straight again.
So now I sent for you, chosen from all,
first that I knew you constant in respect
to Laius' royal power; and again
when Oedipus had set the state to rights,
and when he perished, you were faithful still
in mind to the descendants of the dead.
When they two perished by a double fate,   170
on one day struck and striking and defiled
each by his own hand, now it comes that I

hold all the power and the royal throne
through close connection with the perished men.
You cannot learn of any man the soul,
the mind, and the intent until he shows
his practise of the government and law.
For I believe that who controls the state
and does not hold to the best plans of all,
but locks his tongue up through some kind of fear,   180
that he is worst of all who are or were.
And he who counts another greater friend
than his own fatherland, I put him nowhere.
So I—may Zeus all-seeing always know it—
could not keep silent as disaster crept
upon the town, destroying hope of safety.
Nor could I count the enemy of the land
friend to myself, not I who know so well
that she it is who saves us, sailing straight,
and only so can we have friends at all.   190
With such good rules shall I enlarge our state.
And now I have proclaimed their brother-edict.
In the matter of the sons of Oedipus,
citizens, know: Eteocles who died,
defending this our town with champion spear,
is to be covered in the grave and granted
all holy rites we give the noble dead.
But his brother Polyneices whom I name
the exile who came back and sought to burn   200
his fatherland, the gods who were his kin,
who tried to gorge on blood he shared, and lead
the rest of us as slaves—
it is announced that no one in this town
may give him burial or mourn for him.
Leave him unburied, leave his corpse disgraced,
a dinner for the birds and for the dogs.
Such is my mind. Never shall I, myself,
honor the wicked and reject the just.

The man who is well-minded to the state
from me in death and life shall have his honor.   210

Chorus

This resolution, Creon, is your own,
in the matter of the traitor and the true.
For you can make such rulings as you will
about the living and about the dead.

Creon

Now you be sentinels of the decree.

Chorus

Order some younger man to take this on.

Creon

Already there are watchers of the corpse.

Chorus

What other order would you give us, then?

Creon

Not to take sides with any who disobey.

Chorus

No fool is fool as far as loving death.   220

Creon

Death is the price. But often we have known
men to be ruined by the hope of profit.

                                (Enter, from the side, a guard.)
Guard

Lord, I can't claim that I am out of breath
from rushing here with light and hasty step,
for I had many haltings in my thought
making me double back upon my road.
My mind kept saying many things to me:
"Why go where you will surely pay the price?"
"Fool, are you halting? And if Creon learns
from someone else, how shall you not be hurt?"   230
Turning this over, on I dilly-dallied.

And so a short trip turns itself to long.
Finally, though, my coming here won out.
If what I say is nothing, still I'll say it.
For I come clutching to one single hope
that I can't suffer what is not my fate.

Creon

What is it that brings on this gloom of yours?

Guard

I want to tell you first about myself.
I didn't do it, didn't see who did it.
It isn't right for me to get in trouble.   240

Creon

Your aim is good. You fence the fact around.
It's clear you have some shocking news to tell.

Guard

Terrible tidings make for long delays.

Creon

Speak out the story, and then get away.

Guard

I'll tell you. Someone left the corpse just now,
burial all accomplished, thirsty dust
strewn on the flesh, the ritual complete.

Creon

What are you saying? What man has dared to do it?

Guard

I wouldn't know. There were no marks of picks,
no grubbed-out earth. The ground was dry and hard,   250
no trace of wheels. The doer left no sign.
When the first fellow on the day-shift showed us,
we all were sick with wonder.
For he was hidden, not inside a tomb,
light dust upon him, enough to turn the curse,
no wild beast's track, nor track of any hound

having been near, nor was the body torn.
We roared bad words about, guard against guard,   260
and came to blows. No one was there to stop us.
Each man had done it, nobody had done it
so as to prove it on him—we couldn't tell.
We were prepared to hold to red-hot iron,
to walk through fire, to swear before the gods
we hadn't done it, hadn't shared the plan,
when it was plotted or when it was done.
And last, when all our sleuthing came out nowhere,
one fellow spoke, who made our heads to droop
low toward the ground. We couldn't disagree.   270
We couldn't see a chance of getting off.
He said we had to tell you all about it.
We couldn't hide the fact.
So he won out. The lot chose poor old me
to win the prize. So here I am unwilling,
quite sure you people hardly want to see me.
Nobody likes the bringer of bad news.

Chorus

Lord, while he spoke, my mind kept on debating.
Isn't this action possibly a god's?

Creon

Stop now, before you fill me up with rage,   280
or you'll prove yourself insane as well as old.
Unbearable, your saying that the gods
take any kindly forethought for this corpse.
Would it be they had hidden him away,
honoring his good service, his who came
to burn their pillared temples and their wealth,
even their land, and break apart their laws?
Or have you seen them honor wicked men?
It isn't so.
No, from the first there were some men in town   290
who took the edict hard, and growled against me,

who hid the fact that they were rearing back,
not rightly in the yoke, no way my friends.
These are the people—oh it's clear to me—
who have bribed these men and brought about the deed.
No current custom among men as bad
as silver currency. This destroys the state;
this drives men from their homes; this wicked teacher
drives solid citizens to acts of shame.
It shows men how to practise infamy   300
and know the deeds of all unholiness.
Every least hireling who helped in this
brought about then the sentence he shall have.
But further, as I still revere great Zeus,
understand this, I tell you under oath,
if you don't find the very man whose hands
buried the corpse, bring him for me to see,
not death alone shall be enough for you
till living, hanging, you make clear the crime.
For any future grabbings you'll have learned   310
where to get pay, and that it doesn't pay
to squeeze a profit out of every source.
For you'll have felt that more men come to doom
through dirty profits than are kept by them.

Guard
    May I say something? Or just turn and go?

Creon
    Aren't you aware your speech is most unwelcome?

Guard
    Does it annoy your hearing or your mind?

Creon
    Why are you out to allocate my pain?

Guard
    The doer hurts your mind. I hurt your ears.

Creon

You are a quibbling rascal through and through.　　　　320

Guard

But anyhow I never did the deed.

Creon

And you the man who sold your mind for money!

Guard

Oh!
How terrible to guess, and guess at lies!

Creon

Go pretty up your guesswork. If you don't
show me the doers you will have to say
that wicked payments work their own revenge.

Guard

Indeed, I pray he's found, but yes or no,
taken or not as luck may settle it,
you won't see me returning to this place.
Saved when I neither hoped nor thought to be,　　　　330
I owe the gods a mighty debt of thanks.

　　　(*Creon enters the palace. The Guard leaves by the way he came.*)

Chorus

Many the wonders but nothing walks stranger than man.
This thing crosses the sea in the winter's storm,
making his path through the roaring waves.
And she, the greatest of gods, the earth—
ageless she is, and unwearied—he wears her away
as the ploughs go up and down from year to year　　　　340
and his mules turn up the soil.

Gay nations of birds he snares and leads,
wild beast tribes and the salty brood of the sea,
with the twisted mesh of his nets, this clever man.
He controls with craft the beasts of the open air,
walkers on hills. The horse with his shaggy mane　　　　350

he holds and harnesses, yoked about the neck,
and the strong bull of the mountain.

Language, and thought like the wind
and the feelings that make the town,
he has taught himself, and shelter against the cold,
refuge from rain. He can always help himself.
He faces no future helpless. There's only death
that he cannot find an escape from. He has contrived   360
refuge from illnesses once beyond all cure.

Clever beyond all dreams
the inventive craft that he has
which may drive him one time or another to well or ill.
When he honors the laws of the land and the gods' sworn right
high indeed is his city; but stateless the man   370
who dares to dwell with dishonor. Not by my fire,
never to share my thoughts, who does these things.

                              (*The Guard enters with Antigone.*)
   My mind is split at this awful sight.
   I know her. I cannot deny
   Antigone is here.
   Alas, the unhappy girl,
   her unhappy father's child.
   Oh what is the meaning of this?   380
   It cannot be you that they bring
   for breaking the royal law,
   caught in open shame.

Guard
   This is the woman who has done the deed.
   We caught her at the burying. Where's the king?

                                              (*Creon enters.*)
Chorus
   Back from the house again just when he's needed.

Creon
   What must I measure up to? What has happened?

Guard

Lord, one should never swear off anything.
Afterthought makes the first resolve a liar.
I could have vowed I wouldn't come back here   390
after your threats, after the storm I faced.
But joy that comes beyond the wildest hope
is bigger than all other pleasure known.
I'm here, though I swore not to be, and bring
this girl. We caught her burying the dead.
This time we didn't need to shake the lots;
mine was the luck, all mine.
So now, lord, take her, you, and question her
and prove her as you will. But I am free.
And I deserve full clearance on this charge.   400

Creon

Explain the circumstance of the arrest.

Guard

She was burying the man. You have it all.

Creon

Is this the truth? And do you grasp its meaning?

Guard

I saw her burying the very corpse
you had forbidden. Is this adequate?

Creon

How was she caught and taken in the act?

Guard

It was like this: when we got back again
struck with those dreadful threatenings of yours,
we swept away the dust that hid the corpse.   410
We stripped it back to slimy nakedness.
And then we sat to windward on the hill
so as to dodge the smell.
We poked each other up with growling threats
if anyone was careless of his work.

For some time this went on, till it was noon.
The sun was high and hot. Then from the earth
up rose a dusty whirlwind to the sky,
filling the plain, smearing the forest-leaves,
clogging the upper air. We shut our eyes,   420
sat and endured the plague the gods had sent.
So the storm left us after a long time.
We saw the girl. She cried the sharp and shrill
cry of a bitter bird which sees the nest
bare where the young birds lay.
So this same girl, seeing the body stripped,
cried with great groanings, cried a dreadful curse
upon the people who had done the deed.
Soon in her hands she brought the thirsty dust,
and holding high a pitcher of wrought bronze   430
she poured the three libations for the dead.
We saw this and surged down. We trapped her fast;
and she was calm. We taxed her with the deeds
both past and present. Nothing was denied.
And I was glad, and yet I took it hard.
One's own escape from trouble makes one glad;
but bringing friends to trouble is hard grief.
Still, I care less for all these second thoughts
than for the fact that I myself am safe.   440

Creon
    You there, whose head is drooping to the ground,
    do you admit this, or deny you did it?

Antigone
    I say I did it and I don't deny it.

Creon (to the guard)
    Take yourself off wherever you wish to go
    free of a heavy charge.

Creon (to Antigone)
    You—tell me not at length but in a word.
    You knew the order not to do this thing?

Antigone

I knew, of course I knew. The word was plain.

Creon

And still you dared to overstep these laws?

Antigone

For me it was not Zeus who made that order.   450
Nor did that Justice who lives with the gods below
mark out such laws to hold among mankind.
Nor did I think your orders were so strong
that you, a mortal man, could over-run
the gods' unwritten and unfailing laws.
Not now, nor yesterday's, they always live,
and no one knows their origin in time.
So not through fear of any man's proud spirit
would I be likely to neglect these laws,
draw on myself the gods' sure punishment.
I knew that I must die; how could I not?   460
even without your warning. If I die
before my time, I say it is a gain.
Who lives in sorrows many as are mine
how shall he not be glad to gain his death?
And so, for me to meet this fate, no grief.
But if I left that corpse, my mother's son,
dead and unburied I'd have cause to grieve
as now I grieve not.
And if you think my acts are foolishness
the foolishness may be in a fool's eye.   470

Chorus

The girl is bitter. She's her father's child.
She cannot yield to trouble; nor could he.

Creon

These rigid spirits are the first to fall.
The strongest iron, hardened in the fire,
most often ends in scraps and shatterings.

Small curbs bring raging horses back to terms.
Slave to his neighbor, who can think of pride?
This girl was expert in her insolence   480
when she broke bounds beyond established law.
Once she had done it, insolence the second,
to boast her doing, and to laugh in it.
I am no man and she the man instead
if she can have this conquest without pain.
She is my sister's child, but were she child
of closer kin than any at my hearth,
she and her sister should not so escape
their death and doom. I charge Ismene too.
She shared the planning of this burial.   490
Call her outside. I saw her in the house,
maddened, no longer mistress of herself.
The sly intent betrays itself sometimes
before the secret plotters work their wrong.
I hate it too when someone caught in crime
then wants to make it seem a lovely thing.

Antigone
Do you want more than my arrest and death?

Creon
No more than that. For that is all I need.

Antigone
Why are you waiting? Nothing that you say
fits with my thought. I pray it never will.   500
Nor will you ever like to hear my words.
And yet what greater glory could I find
than giving my own brother funeral?
All these would say that they approved my act
did fear not mute them.
(A king is fortunate in many ways,
and most, that he can act and speak at will.)

Creon
None of these others see the case this way.

Antigone

    They see, and do not say. You have them cowed.

Creon

    And you are not ashamed to think alone? 510

Antigone

    No, I am not ashamed. When was it shame
    to serve the children of my mother's womb?

Creon

    It was not your brother who died against him, then?

Antigone

    Full brother, on both sides, my parents' child.

Creon

    Your act of grace, in his regard, is crime.

Antigone

    The corpse below would never say it was.

Creon

    When you honor him and the criminal just alike?

Antigone

    It was a brother, not a slave, who died.

Creon

    Died to destroy this land the other guarded.

Antigone

    Death yearns for equal law for all the dead.

Creon

    Not that the good and bad draw equal shares. 520

Antigone

    Who knows that this is holiness below?

Creon

    Never the enemy, even in death, a friend.

Antigone

    I cannot share in hatred, but in love.

Creon

    Then go down there, if you must love, and love
the dead. No woman rules me while I live.

                    (Ismene is brought from the palace under guard.)

Chorus

    Look there! Ismene is coming out.
    She loves her sister and mourns,
    with clouded brow and bloodied cheeks,
    tears on her lovely face.   530

Creon

    You, lurking like a viper in the house,
who sucked me dry. I looked the other way
while twin destruction planned against the throne.
Now tell me, do you say you shared this deed?
Or will you swear you didn't even know?

Ismene

    I did the deed, if she agrees I did.
I am accessory and share the blame.

Antigone

    Justice will not allow this. You did not
wish for a part, nor did I give you one.

Ismene

    You are in trouble, and I'm not ashamed   540
to sail beside you into suffering.

Antigone

    Death and the dead, they know whose act it was.
I cannot love a friend whose love is words.

Ismene

    Sister, I pray, don't fence me out from honor,
from death with you, and honor done the dead.

Antigone

    Don't die along with me, nor make your own
that which you did not do. My death's enough.

Ismene

When you are gone what life can be my friend?

Antigone

Love Creon. He's your kinsman and your care.

Ismene

Why hurt me, when it does yourself no good? 550

Antigone

I also suffer, when I laugh at you.

Ismene

What further service can I do you now?

Antigone

To save yourself. I shall not envy you.

Ismene

Alas for me. Am I outside your fate?

Antigone

Yes. For you chose to live when I chose death.

Ismene

At least I was not silent. You were warned.

Antigone

Some will have thought you wiser. Some will not.

Ismene

And yet the blame is equal for us both.

Antigone

Take heart. You live. My life died long ago.
And that has made me fit to help the dead. 560

Creon

One of these girls has shown her lack of sense
just now. The other had it from her birth.

Ismene

Yes, lord. When people fall in deep distress
their native sense departs, and will not stay.

Creon
You chose your mind's distraction when you chose
to work out wickedness with this wicked girl.

Ismene
What life is there for me to live without her?

Creon
Don't speak of her. For she is here no more.

Ismene
But will you kill your own son's promised bride?

Creon
Oh, there are other furrows for his plough.

Ismene
But where the closeness that has bound these two?   570

Creon
Not for my sons will I choose wicked wives.

Ismene
Dear Haemon, your father robs you of your rights.

Creon
You and your marriage trouble me too much.

Ismene
You will take away his bride from your own son?

Creon
Yes. Death will help me break this marriage off.

Chorus
It seems determined that the girl must die.

Creon
You helped determine it. Now, no delay!
Slaves, take them in. They must be women now.
No more free running.
Even the bold will fly when they see Death   580
drawing in close enough to end their life.

(Antigone and Ismene are taken inside.)

Chorus

Fortunate they whose lives have no taste of pain.
For those whose house is shaken by the gods
escape no kind of doom. It extends to all the kin
like the wave that comes when the winds of Thrace
run over the dark of the sea.
The black sand of the bottom is brought from the depth;   590
the beaten capes sound back with a hollow cry.

Ancient the sorrow of Labdacus' house, I know.
Dead men's grief comes back, and falls on grief.
No generation can free the next.
One of the gods will strike. There is no escape.
So now the light goes out
for the house of Oedipus, while the bloody knife   600
cuts the remaining root. Folly and Fury have done this.

What madness of man, O Zeus, can bind your power?
Not sleep can destroy it who ages all,
nor the weariless months the gods have set. Unaged in time
monarch you rule of Olympus' gleaming light.   610
Near time, far future, and the past,
one law controls them all:
any greatness in human life brings doom.

Wandering hope brings help to many men.
But others she tricks from their giddy loves,
and her quarry knows nothing until he has walked into flame.
Word of wisdom it was when someone said,   620
"The bad becomes the good
to him a god would doom."
Only briefly is that one from under doom.

(Haemon enters from the side.)

Here is your one surviving son.
Does he come in grief at the fate of his bride,
in pain that he's tricked of his wedding?   630

Creon

Soon we shall know more than a seer could tell us.
Son, have you heard the vote condemned your bride?
And are you here, maddened against your father,
or are we friends, whatever I may do?

Haemon

My father, I am yours. You keep me straight
with your good judgment, which I shall ever follow.
Nor shall a marriage count for more with me
than your kind leading.

Creon

There's my good boy. So should you hold at heart
and stand behind your father all the way.   640
It is for this men pray they may beget
households of dutiful obedient sons,
who share alike in punishing enemies,
and give due honor to their father's friends.
Whoever breeds a child that will not help
what has he sown but trouble for himself,
and for his enemies laughter full and free?
Son, do not let your lust mislead your mind,
all for a woman's sake, for well you know
how cold the thing he takes into his arms   650
who has a wicked woman for his wife.
What deeper wounding than a friend no friend?
Oh spit her forth forever, as your foe.
Let the girl marry somebody in Hades.
Since I have caught her in the open act,
the only one in town who disobeyed,
I shall not now proclaim myself a liar,
but kill her. Let her sing her song of Zeus
who guards the kindred.
If I allow disorder in my house
I'd surely have to licence it abroad.   660
A man who deals in fairness with his own,

he can make manifest justice in the state.
But he who crosses law, or forces it,
or hopes to bring the rulers under him,
shall never have a word of praise from me.
The man the state has put in place must have
obedient hearing to his least command
when it is right, and even when it's not.
He who accepts this teaching I can trust,
ruler, or ruled, to function in his place,
to stand his ground even in the storm of spears,   670
a mate to trust in battle at one's side.
There is no greater wrong than disobedience.
This ruins cities, this tears down our homes,
this breaks the battle-front in panic-rout.
If men live decently it is because
discipline saves their very lives for them.
So I must guard the men who yield to order,
not let myself be beaten by a woman.
Better, if it must happen, that a man
should overset me.
I won't be called weaker than womankind.   680

Chorus

We think—unless our age is cheating us—
that what you say is sensible and right.

Haemon

Father, the gods have given men good sense,
the only sure possession that we have.
I couldn't find the words in which to claim
that there was error in your late remarks.
Yet someone else might bring some further light.
Because I am your son I must keep watch
on all men's doing where it touches you,
their speech, and most of all, their discontents.
Your presence frightens any common man   690
from saying things you would not care to hear.

But in dark corners I have heard them say
how the whole town is grieving for this girl,
unjustly doomed, if ever woman was,
to die in shame for glorious action done.
She would not leave her fallen, slaughtered brother
there, as he lay, unburied, for the birds
and hungry dogs to make an end of him.
Isn't her real desert a golden prize?
This is the undercover speech in town.   700
Father, your welfare is my greatest good.
What loveliness in life for any child
outweighs a father's fortune and good fame?
And so a father feels his children's faring.
Then, do not have one mind, and one alone
that only your opinion can be right.
Whoever thinks that he alone is wise,
his eloquence, his mind, above the rest,
come the unfolding, shows his emptiness.
A man, though wise, should never be ashamed   710
of learning more, and must unbend his mind.
Have you not seen the trees beside the torrent,
the ones that bend them saving every leaf,
while the resistant perish root and branch?
And so the ship that will not slacken sail,
the sheet drawn tight, unyielding, overturns.
She ends the voyage with her keel on top.
No, yield your wrath, allow a change of stand.
Young as I am, if I may give advice,
I'd say it would be best if men were born   720
perfect in wisdom, but that failing this
(which often fails) it can be no dishonor
to learn from others when they speak good sense.

Chorus

Lord, if your son has spoken to the point
you should take his lesson. He should do the same.
Both sides have spoken well.

Creon
> At my age I'm to school my mind by his?
> This boy instructor is my master, then?

Haemon
> I urge no wrong. I'm young, but you should watch
> my actions, not my years, to judge of me.

Creon
> A loyal action, to respect disorder?   730

Haemon
> I wouldn't urge respect for wickedness.

Creon
> You don't think she is sick with that disease?

Haemon
> Your fellow-citizens maintain she's not.

Creon
> Is the town to tell me how I ought to rule?

Haemon
> Now there you speak just like a boy yourself.

Creon
> Am I to rule by other mind than mine?

Haemon
> No city is property of a single man.

Creon
> But custom gives possession to the ruler.

Haemon
> You'd rule a desert beautifully alone.

Creon (to the Chorus)
> It seems he's firmly on the woman's side.   740

Haemon
> If you're a woman. It is you I care for.

Creon
> Wicked, to try conclusions with your father.

Haemon

When you conclude unjustly, so I must.

Creon

Am I unjust, when I respect my office?

Haemon

You tread down the gods' due. Respect is gone.

Creon

Your mind is poisoned. Weaker than a woman!

Haemon

At least you'll never see me yield to shame.

Creon

Your whole long argument is but for her.

Haemon

And you, and me, and for the gods below.

Creon

You shall not marry her while she's alive.   750

Haemon

Then she shall die. Her death will bring another.

Creon

Your boldness has made progress. Threats, indeed!

Haemon

No threat, to speak against your empty plan.

Creon

Past due, sharp lessons for your empty brain.

Haemon

If you weren't father, I should call you mad.

Creon

Don't flatter me with "father," you woman's slave.

Haemon

You wish to speak but never wish to hear.

Creon

You think so? By Olympus, you shall not
revile me with these tauntings and go free.

Bring out the hateful creature; she shall die
full in his sight, close at her bridegroom's side. 760

Haemon

Not at my side her death, and you will not
ever lay eyes upon my face again.
Find other friends to rave with after this.

(Haemon leaves, by one of the side entrances.)

Chorus

Lord, he has gone with all the speed of rage.
When such a man is grieved his mind is hard.

Creon

Oh, let him go, plan superhuman action.
In any case the girls shall not escape.

Chorus

You plan for both the punishment of death? 770

Creon

Not her who did not do it. You are right.

Chorus

And what death have you chosen for the other?

Creon

To take her where the foot of man comes not.
There shall I hide her in a hollowed cave
living, and leave her just so much to eat
as clears the city from the guilt of death.
There, if she prays to Death, the only god
of her respect, she may manage not to die.
Or she may learn at last and even then
how much too much her labor for the dead. 780

(Creon returns to the palace.)

Chorus

Love unconquered in fight, love who falls on our havings.
You rest in the bloom of a girl's unwithered face.
You cross the sea, you are known in the wildest lairs.

Not the immortal gods can fly,
nor men of a day. Who has you within him is mad.   790

You twist the minds of the just. Wrong they pursue and are
    ruined.
You made this quarrel of kindred before us now.
Desire looks clear from the eyes of a lovely bride:
power as strong as the founded world. ˙
For there is the goddess at play with whom no man can fight.   800

(*Antigone is brought from the palace under guard.*)

Now I am carried beyond all bounds.
My tears will not be checked.
I see Antigone depart
to the chamber where all men sleep.

Antigone

Men of my fathers' land, you see me go
my last journey. My last sight of the sun,
then never again. Death who brings all to sleep   810
takes me alive to the shore
of the river underground.
Not for me was the marriage-hymn, nor will anyone start the
    song
at a wedding of mine. Acheron is my mate.

Chorus

With praise as your portion you go
in fame to the vault of the dead.
Untouched by wasting disease,
not paying the price of the sword,   820
of your own motion you go.
Alone among mortals will you descend
in life to the house of Death.

Antigone

Pitiful was the death that stranger died,
our queen once, Tantalus' daughter. The rock
it covered her over, like stubborn ivy it grew.

Still, as she wastes, the rain
and snow companion her.
Pouring down from her mourning eyes comes the water that
   soaks the stone.   830
My own putting to sleep a god has planned like hers.

Chorus

   God's child and god she was.
   We are born to death.
   Yet even in death you will have your fame,
   to have gone like a god to your fate,
   in living and dying alike.

Antigone

   Laughter against me now. In the name of our fathers' gods,
   could you not wait till I went? Must affront be thrown in my
      face?   840
   O city of wealthy men.
   I call upon Dirce's spring,
   I call upon Thebe's grove in the armored plain,
   to be my witnesses, how with no friend's mourning,
   by what decree I go to the fresh-made prison-tomb.
   Alive to the place of corpses, an alien still,   850
   never at home with the living nor with the dead.

Chorus

   You went to the furthest verge
   of daring, but there you found
   the high foundation of justice, and fell.
   Perhaps you are paying your father's pain.

Antigone

   You speak of my darkest thought, my pitiful father's fame,
   spread through all the world, and the doom that haunts our
      house,   860
   the royal house of Thebes.
   My mother's marriage-bed.
   Destruction where she lay with her husband-son,
   my father. These are my parents and I their child.

I go to stay with them. My curse is to die unwed.
My brother, you found your fate when you found your bride,   870
found it for me as well. Dead, you destroy my life.

Chorus

You showed respect for the dead.
So we for you: but power
is not to be thwarted so.
Your self-sufficiency has brought you down.

Antigone

Unwept, no wedding-song, unfriended, now I go
the road laid down for me.
No longer shall I see this holy light of the sun.   880
No friend to bewail my fate.

(Creon enters from the palace.)

Creon

When people sing the dirge for their own deaths
ahead of time, nothing will break them off
if they can hope that this will buy delay.
Take her away at once, and open up
the tomb I spoke of. Leave her there alone.
There let her choose: death, or a buried life.
No stain of guilt upon us in this case,
but she is exiled from our life on earth.   890

Antigone

O tomb, O marriage-chamber, hollowed out
house that will watch forever, where I go.
To my own people, who are mostly there;
Persephone has taken them to her.
Last of them all, ill-fated past the rest,
shall I descend, before my course is run.
Still when I get there I may hope to find
I come as a dear friend to my dear father,
to you, my mother, and my brother too.
All three of you have known my hand in death.   900
I washed your bodies, dressed them for the grave,

poured out the last libation at the tomb.
Last, Polyneices knows the price I pay
for doing final service to his corpse.
And yet the wise will know my choice was right.
Had I had children or their father dead,
I'd let them moulder. I should not have chosen
in such a case to cross the state's decree.
What is the law that lies behind these words?
One husband gone, I might have found another,
or a child from a new man in first child's place,   910
but with my parents hid away in death,
no brother, ever, could spring up for me.
Such was the law by which I honored you.
But Creon thought the doing was a crime,
a dreadful daring, brother of my heart.
So now he takes and leads me out by force.
No marriage-bed, no marriage-song for me,
and since no wedding, so no child to rear.
I go, without a friend, struck down by fate,
live to the hollow chambers of the dead.   920
What divine justice have I disobeyed?
Why, in my misery, look to the gods for help?
Can I call any of them my ally?
I stand convicted of impiety,
the evidence my pious duty done.
Should the gods think that this is righteousness,
in suffering I'll see my error clear.
But if it is the others who are wrong
I wish them no greater punishment than mine.

Chorus

    The same tempest of mind
    as ever, controls the girl.   930

Creon

    Therefore her guards shall regret
    the slowness with which they move.

Antigone

That word comes close to death.

Creon

You are perfectly right in that.

Antigone

O town of my fathers in Thebe's land,
O gods of our house.
I am led away at last.
Look, leaders of Thebes,
I am last of your royal line.
Look what I suffer, at whose command,
because I respected the right.

   (*Antigone is led away. The slow procession should begin during*
               the preceding passage.)

Chorus

Danaë suffered too.
She went from the light to the brass-built room,
chamber and tomb together. Like you, poor child,
she was of great descent, and more, she held and kept
the seed of the golden rain which was Zeus.
Fate has terrible power.
You cannot escape it by wealth or war.
No fort will keep it out, no ships outrun it.

Remember the angry king,
son of Dryas, who raged at the god and paid,
pent in a rock-walled prison. His bursting wrath
slowly went down. As the terror of madness went,
he learned of his frenzied attack on the god.
Fool, he had tried to stop
the dancing women possessed of god,
the fire of Dionysus, the songs and flutes.

Where the dark rocks divide
sea from sea in Thrace
is Salmydessus whose savage god

940

950

960

970

beheld the terrible blinding wounds
dealt to Phineus' sons by their father's wife.
Dark the eyes that looked to avenge their mother.
Sharp with her shuttle she struck, and blooded her hands.

Wasting they wept their fate,
settled when they were born   980
to Cleopatra, unhappy queen.
She was a princess too, of an ancient house,
reared in the cave of the wild north wind, her father.
Half a goddess but, child, she suffered like you.

*(Enter, from the side Teiresias, the blind prophet,
led by a boy attendant.)*

Teiresias

Elders of Thebes, we two have come one road,
two of us looking through one pair of eyes.
This is the way of walking for the blind.   990

Creon

Teiresias, what news has brought you here?

Teiresias

I'll tell you. You in turn must trust the prophet.

Creon

I've always been attentive to your counsel.

Teiresias

And therefore you have steered this city straight.

Creon

So I can say how helpful you have been.

Teiresias

But now you are balanced on a razor's edge.

Creon

What is it? How I shudder at your words!

Teiresias

You'll know, when you hear the signs that I have marked
I sat where every bird of heaven comes   1000

in my old place of augury, and heard
bird-cries I'd never known. They screeched about
goaded by madness, inarticulate.
I marked that they were tearing one another
with claws of murder. I could hear the wing-beats.
I was afraid, so straight away I tried
burnt sacrifice upon the flaming altar.
No fire caught my offerings. Slimy ooze
dripped on the ashes, smoked and sputtered there.
Gall burst its bladder, vanished into vapor;   1010
the fat dripped from the bones and would not burn.
These are the omens of the rites that failed,
as my boy here has told me. He's my guide
as I am guide to others.
Why has this sickness struck against the state?
Through your decision.
All of the altars of the town are choked
with leavings of the dogs and birds; their feast
was on that fated, fallen Polyneices.
So the gods will have no offering from us,
not prayer, nor flame of sacrifice. The birds   1020
will not cry out a sound I can distinguish,
gorged with the greasy blood of that dead man.
Think of these things, my son. All men may err
but error once committed, he's no fool
nor yet unfortunate, who gives up his stiffness
and cures the trouble he has fallen in.
Stubbornness and stupidity are twins.
Yield to the dead. Why goad him where he lies?
What use to kill the dead a second time?   1030
I speak for your own good. And I am right.
Learning from a wise counsellor is not pain
if what he speaks are profitable words.

Creon
    Old man, you all, like bowmen at a mark,
    have bent your bows at me. I've had my share

of seers. I've been an item in your accounts.
Make profit, trade in Lydian silver-gold,
pure gold of India; that's your chief desire.
But you will never cover up that corpse.
Not if the very eagles tear their food   1040
from him, and leave it at the throne of Zeus.
I wouldn't give him up for burial
in fear of that pollution. For I know
no mortal being can pollute the gods.
O old Teiresias, human beings fall;
the clever ones the furthest, when they plead
a shameful case so well in hope of profit.

Teiresias
Alas!
What man can tell me, has he thought at all . . .

Creon
What hackneyed saw is coming from your lips?

Teiresias
How better than all wealth is sound good counsel.   1050

Creon
And so is folly worse than anything.

Teiresias
And you're infected with that same disease.

Creon
I'm reluctant to be uncivil to a seer . . .

Teiresias
You're that already. You have said I lie.

Creon
Well, the whole crew of seers are money-mad.

Teiresias
And the whole tribe of tyrants grab at gain.

Creon
Do you realize you are talking to a king?

Teiresias
 I know. Who helped you save this town you hold?

Creon
 You're a wise seer, but you love wickedness.

Teiresias
 You'll bring me to speak the unspeakable, very soon.   1060

Creon
 Well, speak it out. But do not speak for profit.

Teiresias
 No, there's no profit in my words for you.

Creon
 You'd better realise that you can't deliver
 my mind, if you should sell it, to the buyer.

Teiresias
 Know well, the sun will not have rolled its course
 many more days, before you come to give
 corpse for these corpses, child of your own loins.
 For you've confused the upper and lower worlds.
 You sent a life to settle in a tomb;
 you keep up here that which belongs below   1070
 the corpse unburied, robbed of its release.
 Not you, nor any god that rules on high
 can claim him now.
 You rob the nether gods of what is theirs.
 So the pursuing horrors lie in wait
 to track you down. The Furies sent by Hades
 and by all gods will even you with your victims.
 Now say that I am bribed! At no far time
 shall men and women wail within your house.
 And all the cities that you fought in war   1080
 whose sons had burial from wild beasts, or dogs,
 or birds that brought the stench of your great wrong
 back to each hearth, they move against you now.
 A bowman, as you said, I send my shafts,

now you have moved me, straight. You'll feel the wound.
Boy, take me home now. Let him spend his rage
on younger men, and learn to calm his tongue,
and keep a better mind than now he does.   1090

                                              (*Exit.*)

Chorus

> Lord, he has gone. Terrible prophecies!
> And since the time when I first grew grey hair
> his sayings to the city have been true.

Creon

> I also know this. And my mind is torn.
> To yield is dreadful. But to stand against him.
> Dreadful to strike my spirit to destruction.

Chorus

> Now you must come to counsel, and take advice.

Creon

> What must I do? Speak, and I shall obey.

Chorus

> Go free the maiden from that rocky house.   1100
> Bury the dead who lies in readiness.

Creon

> This is your counsel? You would have me yield?

Chorus

> Quick as you can. The gods move very fast
> when they bring ruin on misguided men.

Creon

> How hard, abandonment of my desire.
> But I can fight necessity no more.

Chorus

> Do it yourself. Leave it to no one else.

Creon

> I'll go at once. Come, followers, to your work.
> You that are here round up the other fellows.

Take axes with you, hurry to that place
that overlooks us.   1110
Now my decision has been overturned
shall I, who bound her, set her free myself.
I've come to fear it's best to hold the laws
of old tradition to the end of life.

(Exit.)

Chorus

God of the many names, Semele's golden child,
child of Olympian thunder, Italy's lord.
Lord of Eleusis, where all men come   1120
to mother Demeter's plain.
Bacchus, who dwell in Thebes,
by Ismenus' running water,
where wild Bacchic women are at home,
on the soil of the dragon seed.

Seen in the glaring flame, high on the double mount,
with the nymphs of Parnassus at play on the hill,
seen by Kastalia's flowing stream.   1130
You come from the ivied heights,
from green Euboea's shore.
In immortal words we cry
your name, lord, who watch the ways,
the many ways of Thebes.

This is your city, honored beyond the rest,
the town of your mother's miracle-death.
Now, as we wrestle our grim disease,   1140
come with healing step from Parnassus' slope
or over the moaning sea.

Leader in dance of the fire-pulsing stars,
overseer of the voices of night,
child of Zeus, be manifest,
with due companionship of Maenad maids   1150
whose cry is but your name.

(Enter one of those who left with Creon, as messenger.)

« 219 »

Messenger

Neighbors of Cadmus, and Amphion's house,
there is no kind of state in human life
which I now dare to envy or to blame.
Luck sets it straight, and luck she overturns
the happy or unhappy day by day.
No prophecy can deal with men's affairs.   1160
Creon was envied once, as I believe,
for having saved this city from its foes
and having got full power in this land.
He steered it well. And he had noble sons.
Now everything is gone.
Yes, when a man has lost all happiness,
he's not alive. Call him a breathing corpse.
Be very rich at home. Live as a king.
But once your joy has gone, though these are left
they are smoke's shadow to lost happiness.   1170

Chorus

What is the grief of princes that you bring?

Messenger

They're dead. The living are responsible.

Chorus

Who died? Who did the murder? Tell us now.

Messenger

Haemon is gone. One of his kin drew blood.

Chorus

But whose arm struck? His father's or his own?

Messenger

He killed himself. His blood is on his father.

Chorus

Seer, all too true the prophecy you told!

Messenger

This is the state of things. Now make your plans.

(Enter, from the palace, Eurydice.)

Chorus

Eurydice is with us now, I see. 1180
Creon's poor wife. She may have come by chance.
She may have heard something about her son.

Eurydice

I heard your talk as I was coming out
to greet the goddess Pallas with my prayer.
And as I moved the bolts that held the door
I heard of my own sorrow.
I fell back fainting in my women's arms.
But say again just what the news you bring. 1190
I, whom you speak to, have known grief before.

Messenger

Dear lady, I was there, and I shall tell,
leaving out nothing of the true account.
Why should I make it soft for you with tales
to prove myself a liar? Truth is right.
I followed your husband to the plain's far edge,
where Polyneices' corpse was lying still
unpitied. The dogs had torn him all apart. 1200
We prayed the goddess of all journeyings,
and Pluto, that they turn their wrath to kindness,
we gave the final purifying bath,
then burned the poor remains on new-cut boughs,
and heaped a high mound of his native earth.
Then turned we to the maiden's rocky bed,
death's hollow marriage-chamber.
But, still far off, one of us heard a voice
in keen lament by that unblest abode.
He ran and told the master. As Creon came
he heard confusion crying. He groaned and spoke: 1210
"Am I a prophet now, and do I tread
the saddest of all roads I ever trod?
My son's voice crying! Servants, run up close,

stand by the tomb and look, push through the crevice
where we built the pile of rock, right to the entry.
Find out if that is Haemon's voice I hear
or if the gods are tricking me indeed."
We obeyed the order of our mournful master.
In the far corner of the tomb we saw   1220
her, hanging by the neck, caught in a noose
of her own linen veiling.
Haemon embraced her as she hung, and mourned
his bride's destruction, dead and gone below,
his father's actions, the unfated marriage.
When Creon saw him, he groaned terribly,
and went toward him, and called him with lament:
"What have you done, what plan have you caught up,
what sort of suffering is killing you?
Come out, my child, I do beseech you, come!"   1230
The boy looked at him with his angry eyes,
spat in his face and spoke no further word.
He drew his sword, but as his father ran,
he missed his aim. Then the unhappy boy,
in anger at himself, leant on the blade.
It entered, half its length, into his side.
While he was conscious he embraced the maiden,
holding her gently. Last, he gasped out blood,
red blood on her white cheek.
Corpse on a corpse he lies. He found his marriage.   1240
Its celebration in the halls of Hades.
So he has made it very clear to men
that to reject good counsel is a crime.

                              (*Eurydice returns to the house.*)
Chorus
    What do you make of this? The queen has gone
    in silence. We know nothing of her mind.

Messenger
    I wonder at her, too. But we can hope
    that she has gone to mourn her son within

with her own women, not before the town.
She knows discretion. She will do no wrong.   1250

Chorus

I am not sure. This muteness may portend
as great disaster as a loud lament.

Messenger

I will go in and see if some deep plan
hides in her heart's wild pain. You may be right.
There can be heavy danger in mute grief.

(*The messenger goes into the house. Creon enters with his
followers. They are carrying Haemon's body on a bier.*)

Chorus

But look, the king draws near.
His own hand brings
the witness of his crime,
the doom he brought on himself.   1260

Creon

O crimes of my wicked heart,
harshness bringing death.
You see the killer, you see the kin he killed.
My planning was all unblest.
Son, you have died too soon.
Oh, you have gone away
through my fault, not your own.

Chorus

You have learned justice, though it comes too late.   1270

Creon

Yes, I have learned in sorrow. It was a god who struck,
who has weighted my head with disaster; he drove me to wild
    strange ways,
his heavy heel on my joy.
Oh sorrows, sorrows of men.

(*Re-enter the messenger, from a side door of the palace.*)

Messenger

Master, you hold one sorrow in your hands
but you have more, stored up inside the house.   1280

Creon

What further suffering can come on me?

Messenger

Your wife has died. The dead man's mother in deed,
poor soul, her wounds are fresh.

Creon

Hades, harbor of all,
you have destroyed me now.
Terrible news to hear, horror the tale you tell.   1290
I was dead, and you kill me again.
Boy, did I hear you right?
Did you say the queen was dead,
slaughter on slaughter heaped?

> *(The central doors of the palace begin to open.)*

Chorus

Now you can see. Concealment is all over.

> *(The doors are open, and the corpse of Eurydice is revealed.)*

Creon

My second sorrow is here. Surely no fate remains
which can strike me again. Just now, I held my son in my arms.
And now I see her dead.
Woe for the mother and son.   1300

Messenger

There, by the altar, dying on the sword,
her eyes fell shut. She wept her older son
who died before, and this one. Last of all
she cursed you as the killer of her children.

Creon

I am mad with fear. Will no one strike
and kill me with cutting sword?
Sorrowful, soaked in sorrow to the bone!   1310

Messenger
> Yes, for she held you guilty in the death
> of him before you, and the elder dead.

Creon
> How did she die?

Messenger
>   Struck home at her own heart
> when she had heard of Haemon's suffering.

Creon
> This is my guilt, all mine. I killed you, I say it clear.
> Servants, take me away, out of the sight of men.   1320
> I who am nothing more than nothing now.

Chorus
> Your plan is good—if any good is left.
> Best to cut short our sorrow.

Creon
> Let me go, let me go. May death come quick,
> bringing my final day.   1330
> O let me never see tomorrow's dawn.

Chorus
> That is the future's. We must look to now.
> What will be is in other hands than ours.

Creon
> All my desire was in that prayer of mine.

Chorus
> Pray not again. No mortal can escape
> the doom prepared for him.

Creon
> Take me away at once, the frantic man who killed   1340
> my son, against my meaning. I cannot rest.
> My life is warped past cure. My fate has struck me down.

>   (*Creon and his attendants enter the house.*)

Chorus

> Our happiness depends
> on wisdom all the way.
> The gods must have their due.
> Great words by men of pride 1350
> bring greater blows upon them.
> So wisdom comes to the old.

A NOTE ON THE TEXT

THE foregoing is a translation of the text of Jebb's third edition (Cambridge, 1900). In the dialogue, I have tried to bring into English almost all that I thought I saw in the Greek, even though this was to run the risk of a clumsy literalism. In the choruses, I have taken more freedom.

The following are the places where my rendering is of another text than Jebb's.

486 ὁμαιμονεστέρας A, other MSS, and the scholiast in L. ὁμαιμονεστέρα L, as corrected from -αις, Jebb.

The extravagance of imagining the impossible possibility of closer blood kin than a sister seems to me in character for Creon at this point. (For a similar use of language, cf. Aeschylus *Septem* 197.)

519 τούτους MSS and Jebb. ἴσους is recorded by L's scholiast and read by Pearson. Line 520 seems even more pointed if Creon is picking up Antigone's own term to throw at her.

572. This line is Ismene's in all the manuscripts. The only traditional evidence for giving it to Antigone is that the Aldine edition (1502) and Turnebus (1553) gave it to her. These editors may have had manuscript evidence lost to us. But they may also, like most modern editors, including Jebb, have been exercising their own sense of fitness. It is touching to have an Antigone stung from her silence to defend her lover. Further, if the line is not hers, we are faced with an Antigone who never mentions him; and much has been built on this.

The best argument for giving her the line is Creon's reply to it (573). If Ismene has 572 "your marriage" must mean "the marriage you talk of," or words to that effect. This is possible, but the phrase would certainly come out more naturally to Antigone.

Confusions of speakers in stichomythia are many, and I see no possibility of certainty here. It is our misfortune that the line in question is an important one. I have stayed with the manuscripts, which seems to me all one can do.

574. This is Ismene's line in all MSS. Boeckh, followed by Jebb, gave it to the chorus. I have followed my own precedent in 572, and stayed with the MSS. The question might come, as Jebb argues, more reasonably from the chorus than from Ismene, who has had her answer already. But she is not too logical to ask the same appalling question twice.

600 κόνις MSS, Jebb. κοπίς Reiske and others, Jebb in earlier editions, Pearson. See Jebb's note and appendix. He was of two minds here. My own final feeling is that for dust to be doing the reaping is too much, even for a tragic chorus.

609 παντογήρως L, the MSS generally, L's scholiast. παντ' ἀγρεύων, Jebb. This image was too strained for Jebb (and many others), as the dust in 600 was for me. De gustibus. . . .

904–20. Jebb (following and followed by many) brackets these lines, which are in all the MSS, and were known to Aristotle as Antigone's. I think he is wrong, but he should not be pilloried as a prudish Victorian for this. The positions of his note and appendix are well taken and held. Some sensible contemporaries (e.g., Fitts and Fitzgerald) are with him still. For those, like myself, who are sure the lines are Antigone's, there is drama in her abandoning her moralities and clinging to her irrational profundity of feeling for her lost and irreplaceable brother, devising legalistic arguments for her intellectual justification. Jebb finds the syntax of 909–12 strained past all bearing, but I believe Antigone's obscurity here a touch of realism parallel to the confused and contradictory negatives of her opening lines, which Jebb allows her.

HIPPOLYTUS

Translated by David Grene

INTRODUCTION

Hippolytus was presented in 428 B.C. and won first prize. It is, however, a second version; a previous *Hippolytus* (lost) had been considered "scandalous" and was badly received. Sophocles used the same story in his *Phaedra*. This is lost, and there is no clue to its date. Seneca in his *Phaedra*, Racine in his *Phèdre*, O'Neill in his *Desire under the Elms*, and Jeffers in his *Cawdor* have, in their own ways, retold the story.

Theseus, king of Athens, had an illegitimate son by an Amazon, Hippolytus. Late in life he married a young wife, Phaedra, princess of Crete, who bore him two sons. Phaedra fell in love with Hippolytus, and her desire was communicated to him. He rejected it, and Phaedra (in this version, by means of a suicide note) told Theseus that Hippolytus had attacked her. Theseus caused his son's death by praying to his own father, Poseidon, to destroy him. But Artemis revealed the truth and established the cult of Hippolytus as a divinity of nature.

This story of the young man tempted and traduced has many parallels in Greek legend, and also in the biblical story of Joseph and the wife of Potiphar. The parallels, however, involve the prompt vindication of the hero and launch him on a career of heroic exploits. The woman in the case figures only as a temptress. Euripides has gone with great sympathy into the feelings of Phaedra, a helpless victim of her passions (Aphrodite) whose mind clings despite all to its integrity. Hippolytus too has his ideals. His seraphic love for the unattainable goddess Artemis displays at the same time his admiration for beauty and his dislike of sex. But the quarrel between sacred and profane love, represented by Artemis and Aphrodite, thwarts the good purposes of the human persons and wrecks both lives.

CHARACTERS

Theseus

Hippolytus, his son by the queen of the Amazons

Phaedra, Theseus' wife, stepmother to Hippolytus

A Servant

A Messenger

The Nurse

The Chorus of Palace women, natives of Troezen

A Chorus of huntsmen, in attendance on Hippolytus

The Goddess Aphrodite

The Goddess Artemis

HIPPOLYTUS

SCENE: *Troezen, in front of the house of Theseus.*

PROLOGUE

Aphrodite

    I am called the Goddess Cypris:
    I am mighty among men and they honor me by many names.
    All those that live and see the light of sun
    from Atlas' Pillars to the tide of Pontus
    are mine to rule.   5
    Such as worship my power in all humility,
    I exalt in honor.
    But those whose pride is stiff-necked against me
    I lay by the heels.
    There is joy in the heart of a God also
    when honored by men.

    Now I will quickly tell you the truth of this story.

    Hippolytus, son of Theseus by the Amazon,   10
    pupil of holy Pittheus,
    alone among the folk of this land of Troezen has blasphemed me
    counting me vilest of the Gods in Heaven.
    He will none of the bed of love nor marriage,
    but honors Artemis, Zeus's daughter,   15
    counting her greatest of the Gods in Heaven
    he is with her continually, this Maiden Goddess, in the greenwood.
    They hunt with hounds and clear the land of wild things,
    mortal with immortal in companionship.
    I do not grudge him such privileges: why should I?   20
    But for his sins against me
    I shall punish Hippolytus this day.
    I have no need to toil to win my end:
    much of the task has been already done.

Once he came from Pittheus' house¹ to the country of Pandion
that he might see and be initiate in the holy mysteries.   25
Phaedra saw him
and her heart was filled with the longings of love.
This was my work.
So before ever she came to Troezen
close to the rock of Pallas in view of this land,   30
she dedicated a temple to Cypris.
For her love, too, dwelt in a foreign land.
Ages to come will call this temple after him,
the temple of the Goddess established here.
When Theseus left the land of Cecrops,
flying from the guilty stain of the murder of the Pallantids,   35
condemning himself to a year's exile
he sailed with his wife to this land.
Phaedra groans in bitterness of heart
and the goads of love prick her cruelly,
and she is like to die.
But she breathes not a word of her secret and none of the servants   40
know of the sickness that afflicts her.
But her love shall not remain thus aimless and unknown.
I will reveal the matter to Theseus and all shall come out.
Father shall slay son with curses—
this son that is hateful to me.
For once the Lord Poseidon, Ruler of the Sea,
granted this favor to Theseus   45
that three of his prayers to the God should find answer.

1. "Pittheus' house": The historian Pausanias, relating the legend of Hippolytus,
says: "King Theseus, when he married Phaedra, daughter of the king of Crete, was in
a quandary what to do with Hippolytus, his son by his former mistress, Antiope the
Amazon. He did not wish that after his own death Hippolytus should rule the children
of his legitimate marriage, nor yet that Hippolytus should be ruled by them, for he
loved him. So he sent the boy to be brought up by his grandfather Pittheus, who lived
in Troezen and ruled there. Theseus hoped that when Pittheus died, Hippolytus might
inherit the kingdom, and thus peace within the family be preserved, Hippolytus gov-
erning Troezen, and Phaedra's children holding sway in Athens." "Pandion's country"
and "land of Cecrops" both signify Attica. Pandion and Cecrops were early legendary
heroes of Attica.

Renowned shall Phaedra be in her death, but none the less
die she must.
Her suffering does not weigh in the scale so much
that I should let my enemies go untouched
escaping payment of that retribution
that honor demands that I have.   50
Look, here is the son of Theseus, Hippolytus!
He has just left his hunting.
I must go away.
See the great crowd that throngs upon his heels
and shouts the praise of Artemis in hymns!   55
He does not know
that the doors of death are open for him,
that he is looking on his last sun.

SCENE I

(Enter Hippolytus, attended by friends and servants carrying
nets, hunting spears, etc.)

Hippolytus

Follow me singing
the praises of Artemis,
Heavenly One, Child of Zeus,
Artemis!
We are the wards of your care.   60

(The Chorus of huntsmen chant.)

Hail, Holy and Gracious!
Hail, Daughter of Zeus!
Hail, Maiden Daughter of Zeus and Leto!   65
Dweller in the spacious sky!
Maid of the Mighty Father!
Maid of the Golden Glistening House!
Hail!
Maiden Goddess most beautiful of all the Heavenly Host that
lives in Olympus!   70

(Hippolytus advances to the altar of Artemis and
lays a garland on it, praying.)

My Goddess Mistress, I bring you ready woven
this garland. It was I that plucked and wove it,
plucked it for you in your inviolate Meadow.
No shepherd dares to feed his flock within it: 75
no reaper plies a busy scythe within it:
only the bees in springtime haunt the inviolate Meadow.
Its gardener is the spirit Reverence who
refreshes it with water from the river.
Not those who by instruction have profited
to learn, but in whose very soul the seed   80
of Chastity toward all things alike
nature has deeply rooted, they alone
may gather flowers there! the wicked may not.

Loved mistress, here I offer you this coronal;
it is a true worshipper's hand that gives it you
to crown the golden glory of your hair.
With no man else I share this privilege
that I am with you and to your words   85
can answer words. True, I may only hear:
I may not see God face to face.
So may I turn the post set at life's end
even as I began the race.

Servant

King—for I will not call you "Master," that belongs
to the Gods only—will you take good advice?

Hippolytus

Certainly I will take good advice. I am not a fool.   90

Servant

In men's communities one rule holds good,
do you know it, King?

Hippolytus

                                   Not I. What is this rule?

Servant

Men hate the haughty of heart who will not be
the friend of every man.

Hippolytus

And rightly too:
For haughty heart breeds arrogant demeanor.

Servant

And affability wins favor, then?   95

Hippolytus

Abundant favor. Aye, and profit, too,
at little cost of trouble.

Servant

Do you think
that it's the same among the Gods in Heaven?

Hippolytus

If we in our world and the Gods in theirs
know the same usages—Yes.

Servant

Then, King, how comes it
that for a holy Goddess you have not even
a word of salutation?

Hippolytus

Which Goddess?
Be careful, or you will find that tongue of yours   100
may make a serious mistake.

Servant

This Goddess here
who stands before your gates, the Goddess Cypris.

Hippolytus

I worship her—but from a long way off,
for I am chaste.

Servant

Yet she's a holy Goddess,
and fair is her renown throughout the world.

Hippolytus

Men make their choice: one man honors one God,
and one another.

Servant

                    Well, good fortune guard you!
if you have the mind you should have.   105

Hippolytus

God of nocturnal prowess is not my God.

Servant

The honors of the Gods you must not scant, my son.

Hippolytus

Go, men, into the house and look to supper.
A plentiful table is an excellent thing
after the hunt. And you (*singling out two*) rub down my horses.   110
When I have eaten I shall exercise them.
For your Cypris here—a long goodbye to her!

                    (*The old man is left standing alone on the stage.*
                    He prays before the statue of Aphrodite.)

O Cypris Mistress, we must not imitate
the young men when they have such thoughts as these.
As fits a slave to speak, here at your image   115
I bow and worship. You should grant forgiveness
when one that has a young tempestuous heart
speaks foolish words. Seem not to hear them.
You should be wiser than mortals, being Gods.   120

                    (*Enter Chorus of women, servants in Phaedra's house.*)

Chorus

                    STROPHE

There is a rock streaming with water,
whose source, men say, is Ocean,
and it pours from the heart of its stone a spring
where pitchers may dip and be filled.
My friend was there and in the river water   125
she dipped and washed the royal purple robes,
and spread them on the rock's warm back
where the sunbeams played,

It was from her I heard at first
of the news of my mistress' sorrow.   130

ANTISTROPHE

She lies on her bed within the house,
within the house and fever wracks her
and she hides her golden head in fine-spun robes.
This is the third day   135
she has eaten no bread
and her body is pure and fasting.
For she would willingly bring her life to anchor
at the end of its voyage
the gloomy harbor of death.   140

STROPHE

Is it Pan's frenzy that possesses you
or is Hecate's madness upon you, maid?
Can it be the holy Corybantes,
or the mighty Mother who rules the mountains?
Are you wasted in suffering thus,   145
for a sin against Dictynna, Queen of hunters?
Are you perhaps unhallowed, having offered
no sacrifice to her from taken victims?
For she goes through the waters of the Lake[2]
can travel on dry land beyond the sea,
the eddying salt sea.   .   150

ANTISTROPHE

Can it be that some other woman's love,
a secret love that hides itself from you,
has beguiled your husband
the son of Erechtheus
our sovran lord, that prince of noble birth?
Or has some sailor from the shores of Crete   155

2. Limnae, the Lake, a district in Laconia, was the center of the worship of Artemis
in the Peloponnese. From it she is sometimes called Limnaios, or Lady of the Lake.

put in at this harbor hospitable to sailors,
bearing a message for our queen,
and so because he told her some calamity
her spirit is bound in chains of grief
and she lies on her bed in sorrow?   160

EPODE

Unhappy is the compound of woman's nature;
the torturing misery of helplessness,
the helplessness of childbirth and its madness
are linked to it for ever.
My body, too, has felt this thrill of pain,   165
and I called on Artemis, Queen of the Bow;
she has my reverence always
as she goes in the company of the Gods.

But here is the old woman, the queen's nurse   170
here at the door. She is bringing her mistress out.
There is a gathering cloud upon her face.
What is the matter? my soul is eager to know.
What can have made the queen so pale?
What can have wasted her body so?   175

SCENE II

(Enter the Nurse, supporting Phaedra.)

Nurse

A weary thing is sickness and its pains!
What must I do now?
Here is light and air, the brightness of the sky.
I have brought out the couch on which you tossed
in fever—here clear of the house.   180
Your every word has been to bring you out,
but when you're here, you hurry in again.
You find no constant pleasure anywhere
for when your joy is upon you, suddenly
you're foiled and cheated.
There's no content for you in what you have
for you're forever finding something dearer,

some other thing—because you have it not.   185
It's better to be sick than nurse the sick.
Sickness is single trouble for the sufferer:
but nursing means vexation of the mind,
and hard work for the hands besides.
The life of man entire is misery:
he finds no resting place, no haven from calamity.   190
But something other dearer still than life
the darkness hides and mist encompasses;
we are proved luckless lovers of this thing
that glitters in the underworld: no man
can tell us of the stuff of it, expounding   195
what is, and what is not: we know nothing of it.
Idly we drift, on idle stories carried.

Phaedra (to the servants)

Lift me up! Lift my head up! All the muscles
are slack and useless. Here, you, take my hands.
They're beautiful, my hands and arms!   200
Take away this hat! It is too heavy to wear.
Take it away! Let my hair fall free on my shoulders.

Nurse

Quiet, child, quiet! Do not so restlessly
keep tossing to and fro! It's easier
to bear an illness if you have some patience   205
and the spirit of good breeding.
We all must suffer sometimes: we are mortal.

Phaedra

O,
if I could only draw from the dewy spring
a draught of fresh spring water!
If I could only lie beneath the poplars,   210
in the tufted meadow and find my rest there!

Nurse

Child, why do you rave so? There are others here.

Cease tossing out these wild demented words
whose driver is madness.

Phaedra

Bring me to the mountains! I *will* go to the mountains!   215
Among the pine trees where the huntsmen's pack
trails spotted stags and hangs upon their heels.
God, how I long to set the hounds on, shouting!
And poise the Thessalian javelin drawing it back—
here where my fair hair hangs above the ear—   220
I would hold in my hand a spear with a steel point.

Nurse

What ails you, child? What is this love of hunting,
and you a lady! Draught of fresh spring water!
Here, beside the tower there is a sloping ridge   225
with springs enough to satisfy your thirst.

Phaedra

Artemis, mistress of the Salty Lake,
mistress of the ring echoing to the racers' hoofs,
if only I could gallop your level stretches,   230
and break Venetian colts!

Nurse

This is sheer madness,
that prompts such whirling, frenzied, senseless words.
Here at one moment you're afire with longing
to hunt wild beasts and you'd go to the hills,
and then again all your desire is horses,
horses on the sands beyond the reach of the breakers.   235
Indeed, it would need to be a mighty prophet
to tell which of the Gods mischievously
jerks you from your true course and thwarts your wits!

Phaedra

O, I am miserable! What is this I've done?
Where have I strayed from the highway of good sense?   240
I was mad. It was the madness sent from some God

that caused my fall.
I am unhappy, so unhappy! Nurse,
cover my face again. I am ashamed   245
of what I said. Cover me up. The tears
are flowing, and my face is turned to shame.
Rightness of judgment is bitterness to the heart.
Madness is terrible. It is better then
that I should die and know no more of anything.

Nurse

There, now, you are covered up. But my own body   250
when will death cover that? I have learned much
from my long life. The mixing bowl of friendship,
the love of one for the other, must be tempered.
Love must not touch the marrow of the soul.   255
Our affections must be breakable chains that we
can cast them off or tighten them.
That one soul so for two should be in travail
as I for her, that is a heavy burden.   260
The ways of life that are most fanatical
trip us up more, they say, than bring us joy.
They're enemies to health. So I praise less
the extreme than temperance in everything,   265
The wise will bear me out.

Chorus Leader

Old woman, you are Phaedra's faithful nurse.
We can see that she is in trouble but the cause
that ails her is black mystery to us.
We would like to hear you tell us what is the matter.   270

Nurse

I have asked and know no more. She will not tell me.

Chorus Leader

Not even what began it?

Nurse

                    And my answer
is still the same: of all this she will not speak.

Chorus Leader

But see how ill she is, and how her body
is wracked and wasted!

Nurse

Yes, she has eaten nothing
for two days now.   275

Chorus Leader

Is this the scourge of madness?
Or can it be . . . that death is what she seeks?

Nurse

Aye, death. She is starving herself to death.

Chorus Leader

I wonder that her husband suffers this.

Nurse

She hides her troubles, swears that she isn't sick.

Chorus Leader

But does he not look into her face and see   280
a witness that disproves her?

Nurse

No, he is gone.
He is away from home, in foreign lands.

Chorus Leader

Why, you must force her then to find the cause
of this mind-wandering sickness!

Nurse

Every means
I have tried and still have won no foot of ground.
But I'll not give up trying, even now.   285
You are here and can in person bear me witness
that I am loyal to my masters always,
even in misfortune's hour.
Dear child, let us both forget our former words.
Be kinder, you: unknit that ugly frown.

For my part I will leave this track of thought: 290
I cannot understand you there. I'll take
another and a better argument.

If you are sick and it is some secret sickness,
here are women standing at your side to help.
But if your troubles may be told to men,   295
speak, that a doctor may pronounce upon it.
So, not a word! Oh, why will you not speak?
There is no remedy in silence, child.
Either I am wrong and then you should correct me:
or right, and you should yield to what I say.
Say something! Look at me!   300

Women, I have tried and tried and all for nothing.
We are as far as ever from our goal.
It was the same before. She was not melted
by anything I said. She would not obey me.

But this you shall know, though to my reasoning
you are more dumbly obstinate than the sea:
If you die, you will be a traitor to your children.   305
They will never know their share in a father's palace.
No, by the Amazon Queen, the mighty rider
who bore a master for your children, one
bastard in birth but true-born son in mind,
you know him well—Hippolytus. . . .
                        So that has touched you?   310

Phaedra

You have killed me, nurse. For God's sake, I entreat you,
never again speak that man's name to me.

Nurse

You see? You have come to your senses, yet despite that,
you will not make your children happy nor
save your own life besides.

Phaedra

I love my children.
It is another storm of fate that batters me.   315

Nurse

There is no stain of blood upon your hands?

Phaedra

My hands are clean: the stain is in my heart.

Nurse

The hurt comes from outside? Some enemy?

Phaedra

One I love destroys me. Neither of us wills it.

Nurse

Has Theseus sinned a sin against you then?   320

Phaedra

God keep me equally guiltless in his sight!

Nurse

What is this terror urging you to death?

Phaedra

Leave me to my sins. My sins are not against you.

Nurse

Not of my will, but yours, you cast me off.

Phaedra

Would you force confession, my hand-clasping suppliant?   325

Nurse

Your knees too—and my hands will never free you.

Phaedra

Sorrow, nurse, sorrow, you will find my secret.

Nurse

Can I know greater sorrow than losing you?

Phaedra

You will kill me. My honor lies in silence.

Nurse

And then you will hide this honor, though I beseech you? 330

Phaedra

Yes, for I seek to win good out of shame.

Nurse

Where honor is, speech will make you more honorable.

Phaedra

O God, let go my hand and go away!

Nurse

No, for you have not given me what you should.

Phaedra

I yield. Your suppliant hand compels my reverence. 335

Nurse

I will say no more. Yours is the word from now.

Phaedra

Unhappy mother, what a love was yours!

Nurse

It is her love for the bull you mean, dear child?

Phaedra

Unhappy sister, bride of Dionysus!

Nurse

Why these ill-boding words about your kin? 340

Phaedra

And I the unlucky third, see how I end!

Nurse

Your words are wounds. Where will your tale conclude?

Phaedra

Mine is an inherited curse. It is not new.

Nurse

I have not yet heard what I most want to know.

Phaedra

If you could say for me what I must say for myself.   345

Nurse

I am no prophet to know your hidden secrets.

Phaedra

What is this thing, this love, of which they speak?

Nurse

Sweetest and bitterest, both in one, at once.

Phaedra

One of the two, the bitterness, I've known.

Nurse

Are you in love, my child? And who is he?   350

Phaedra

There is a man, . . . his mother was an Amazon. . . .

Nurse

You mean Hippolytus?

Phaedra
                          You
have spoken it, not I.

Nurse

What do you mean? This is my death.
Women, this is past bearing. I'll not bear
life after this. A curse upon the daylight!
A curse upon this shining sun above us!   355
I'll throw myself from a cliff, throw myself headlong!
I'll be rid of life somehow, I'll die somehow!
Farewell to all of you! This is the end for me.

The chaste, they love not vice of their own will,
but yet they love it. Cypris, you are no God.

You are something stronger than God if that can be.   360
You have ruined her and me and all this house.

(*The Nurse goes off. The Chorus forms into two half-choruses.*)

First Half-chorus

Did you hear, did you hear
the queen crying aloud,
telling of a calamity
which no ear should hear?

Second Half-chorus

I would rather die
than think such thoughts as hers.   365

First Half-chorus

I am sorry for her trouble.

Second Half-chorus

Alas for troubles, man-besetting.

First Half-chorus (*turning to Phaedra*)

You are dead, you yourself
have dragged your ruin to the light.
What can happen now in the long
dragging stretch of the rest of your days?
Some new thing will befall the house.   370

Chorus (*united*)

We know now, we know now
how your love will end,
poor unhappy Cretan girl!

Phaedra

Hear me, you women of Troezen who live
in this extremity of land, this anteroom to Argos.
Many a time in night's long empty spaces   375
I have pondered on the causes of a life's shipwreck.
I think that our lives are worse than the mind's quality
would warrant. There are many who know virtue.

We know the good, we apprehend it clearly.   380
But we can't bring it to achievement. Some
are betrayed by their own laziness, and others
value some other pleasure above virtue.
There are many pleasures in a woman's life—
long gossiping talks and leisure, that sweet curse.
Then there is shame that thwarts us. Shame is of two kinds.   385
The one is harmless, but the other a plague.
For clarity's sake, we should not talk of "shame,"
a single word for two quite different things.
These then are my thoughts. Nothing can now seduce me   390
to the opposite opinion. I will tell you
in my own case the track which my mind followed.
At first when love had struck me, I reflected
how best to bear it. Silence was my first plan.
Silence and concealment. For the tongue
is not to be trusted: it can criticize   395
another's faults, but on its own possessor
it brings a thousand troubles.
Then I believed that I could conquer love,
conquer it with discretion and good sense.
And when that too failed me, I resolved to die.   400
And death is the best plan of them all. Let none of you
dispute that.
It would always be my choice
to have my virtues known and honored. So
when I do wrong I could not endure to see
a circle of condemning witnesses.
I know what I have done: I know the scandal: 405
and all too well I know that I am a woman,
object of hate to all. Destruction light
upon the wife who herself plays the tempter
and strains her loyalty to her husband's bed
by dalliance with strangers. In the wives   410
of noble houses first this taint begins:
when wickedness approves itself to those

of noble birth, it will surely be approved
by their inferiors. Truly, too, I hate
lip-worshippers of chastity who own
a lecherous daring when they have privacy.
O Cypris, Sea-Born Goddess, how can they   415
look frankly in the faces of their husbands
and never shiver with fear lest their accomplice,
the darkness, and the rafters of the house
take voice and cry aloud?
This then, my friends, is my destruction:
I cannot bear that I should be discovered   420
a traitor to my husband and my children.
God grant them rich and glorious life in Athens—
famous Athens—freedom in word and deed,
and from their mother an honorable name.
It makes the stoutest-hearted man a slave
if in his soul he knows his parents' shame.   425

The proverb runs: "There is one thing alone
that stands the brunt of life throughout its course,
a quiet conscience," . . . a just and quiet conscience
whoever can attain it.
Time holds a mirror, as for a young girl,
and sometimes as occasion falls, he shows us
the ugly rogues of the world. I would not wish
that I should be seen among them.   430

Chorus Leader

How virtue is held lovely everywhere,
and harvests a good name among mankind!

(*The Nurse returns.*)

Nurse

Mistress, the trouble you have lately told me,
coming on me so suddenly, frightened me;
but now I realize that I was foolish.   435
In this world second thoughts, it seems, are best.
Your case is not so extraordinary,

beyond thought or reason. The Goddess in her anger
has smitten you, and you are in love. What wonder
is this? There are many thousands suffer with you.
So, you will die for love! And all the others, 440
who love, and who will love, must they die, too?
How will that profit them? The tide of love,
at its full surge, is not withstandable.
Upon the yielding spirit she comes gently,
but to the proud and the fanatic heart 445
she is a torturer with the brand of shame.
She wings her way through the air; she is in the sea,
in its foaming billows; from her everything,
that is, is born. For she engenders us
and sows the seed of desire whereof we're born, 450
all we her children, living on the earth.
He who has read the writings of the ancients
and has lived much in books, he knows
that Zeus once loved the lovely Semele;
he knows that Dawn, the bright light of the world,
once ravished Cephalus hence to the God's company 455
for love's sake. Yet all these dwell in heaven.
They are content, I am sure, to be subdued
by the stroke of love.
But you, you won't submit! Why, you should certainly
have had your father beget you on fixed terms 460
or with other Gods for masters, if you don't like
the laws that rule this world. Tell me, how many
of the wise ones of the earth do you suppose
see with averted eyes their wives turned faithless;
how many erring sons have fathers helped
with secret loves? It is the wise man's part 465
to leave in darkness everything that is ugly.

We should not in the conduct of our lives
be too exacting. Look, see this roof here—
these overarching beams that span your house—

could builders with all their skill lay them dead straight?
You've fallen into the great sea of love
and with your puny swimming would escape!   470
If in the sum you have more good luck than ill,
count yourself fortunate—for you are mortal.

Come, dear, give up your discontented mood.
Give up your railing. It's only insolent pride
to wish to be superior to the Gods.   475
Endure your love. The Gods have willed it so.
You are sick. Then try to find some subtle means
to turn your sickness into health again.
There are magic love charms, spells of enchantment;
we'll find some remedy for your love-sickness.
Men would take long to hunt devices out,   480
if we the women did not find them first.

Chorus Leader

Phaedra, indeed she speaks more usefully
for today's troubles. But it is you I praise.
And yet my praise brings with it more discomfort
than her words: it is bitterer to the ear.   485

Phaedra

This is the deadly thing which devastates
well-ordered cities and the homes of men—
that's it, this art of oversubtle words.
It's not the words ringing delight in the ear
that one should speak, but those that have the power
to save their hearer's honorable name.

Nurse

This is high moralizing! What you want   490
is not fine words, but the man! Come, let's be done.
And tell your story frankly and directly.
For if there were no danger to your life,
as now there is—or if you could be prudent,
I never would have led you on so far,   495

merely to please your fancy or your lust.
But now a great prize hangs on our endeavors,
and that's the saving of a life—yours, Phaedra,
there's none can blame us for our actions now.

Phaedra

What you say is wicked, wicked! Hold your tongue!
I will not hear such shameful words again.

Nurse

O, they are shameful! But they are better than   500
your noble-sounding moral sentiments.
"The deed" is better if it saves your life:
than your "good name" in which you die exulting.

Phaedra

For God's sake, do not press me any further!
What you say is true, but terrible!
My very soul is subdued by my love
and if you plead the cause of wrong so well   505
I shall fall into the abyss
from which I now am flying.

Nurse

If that is what you think, you should be virtuous.
But if you are not, obey me: that is next best.
It has just come to my mind, I have at home   510
some magic love charms. They will end your trouble;
they'll neither harm your honor nor your mind.
They'll end your trouble, . . . only you must be brave.   515

Phaedra

Is this a poison ointment or a drink?

Nurse

I don't know. Don't be overanxious, child,
to find out what it is. Accept its benefits.

Phaedra

I am afraid of you: I am afraid
that you will be too clever for my good.

Nurse

You are afraid of everything. What is it?

Phaedra

You surely will not tell this to Hippolytus?   520

Nurse

Come, let that be: I will arrange all well.
Only, my lady Cypris of the Sea,
be my helper you. The other plans I have
I'll tell to those we love within the house;
that will suffice.

(*The Nurse goes off.*)

Chorus

STROPHE

Love distills desire upon the eyes,   525
love brings bewitching grace into the heart
of those he would destroy.
I pray that love may never come to me
with murderous intent,
in rhythms measureless and wild.
Not fire nor stars have stronger bolts   530
than those of Aphrodite sent
by the hand of Eros, Zeus's child.

ANTISTROPHE

In vain by Alpheus' stream,   535
in vain in the halls of Phoebus' Pythian shrine
the land of Greece increases sacrifice.
But Love the King of Men they honor not,   540
although he keeps the keys
of the temple of desire,
although he goes destroying through the world,
author of dread calamities
and ruin when he enters human hearts.

STROPHE

The Oechalian maiden who had never known   545
the bed of love, known neither man nor marriage,

the Goddess Cypris gave to Heracles.
She took her from the home of Eurytus,
maiden unhappy in her marriage song,
wild as a Naiad or a Bacchanal,   550
with blood and fire, a murderous hymenaeal!

ANTISTROPHE

O holy walls of Thebes and Dirce's fountain   555
bear witness you, to Love's grim journeying:
once you saw Love bring Semele to bed,
lull her to sleep, clasped in the arms of Death,
pregnant with Dionysus by the thunder king.   560
Love is like a flitting bee in the world's garden
and for its flowers, destruction is in his breath.

SCENE III

(Phaedra is standing listening near the central door of the palace.)

Phaedra

Women, be silent!

(She listens and then recoils.)

Oh, I am destroyed forever.   565

Chorus Leader

What is there terrible within the house?

Phaedra

Hush, let me hear the voices within!

Chorus Leader

And I obey. But this is sorrow's prelude.

Phaedra *(cries out)*

Oh, I am the most miserable of women!   570

*(The Chorus Leader and the Chorus babble
excitedly among themselves.)*

What does she mean by her cries?
Why does she scream?
Tell us the fear-winged word, Mistress, the fear-winged word,
rushing upon the heart.

Phaedra

I am lost. Go, women, stand and listen there yourselves   575
and hear the tumult that falls on the house.

Chorus Leader

Mistress, you stand at the door.
It is you who can tell us best
what happens within the house.   580

Phaedra

Only the son of the horse-loving Amazon,
Hippolytus, cursing a servant maid.

Chorus Leader

My ears can catch a sound,   585
but I can hear nothing clear.
I can only hear a voice
scolding in anger.

Phaedra

It is plain enough. He cries aloud against
the mischievous bawd who betrays her mistress' love.   590

Chorus Leader

Lady, you are betrayed!
How can I help you?
What is hidden is revealed.
You are destroyed.
Those you love have betrayed you.   595

Phaedra

She loved me and she told him of my troubles,
and so has ruined me. She was my doctor,
but her cure has made my illness mortal now.

Chorus Leader

What will you do? There is no cure.

Phaedra

I know of one, and only one—quick death.
That is the only cure for my disease.   600

(*She retires into the palace through one of the side doors just as Hippolytus issues through the central door, dogged by the Nurse. Phaedra is conceived of as listening from behind her door during the entire conversation between the Nurse and Hippolytus.*)

Hippolytus

O Mother Earth! O Sun and open sky!
What words I have heard from this accursed tongue!

Nurse

Hush, son! Someone may hear you.

Hippolytus

You cannot
expect that I hear horror and stay silent.

Nurse

I beg of you, entreat you by your right hand,
your strong right hand, . . . don't speak of this!   605

Hippolytus

Don't lay your hand on me! Let go my cloak!

Nurse

By your knees then, . . . don't destroy me!

Hippolytus

What is this?
Don't you declare that you have done nothing wrong?

Nurse

Yes, but the story, son, is not for everyone.

Hippolytus

Why not? A pleasant tale makes pleasanter telling,
when there are many listeners.   610

Nurse

You will not break your oath to me, surely you will not?

Hippolytus

My tongue swore, but my mind was still unpledged.

Nurse

Son, what would you do?
You'll not destroy your friends?

Hippolytus

"Friends" you say!
I spit the word away. None of the wicked
are friends of mine.

Nurse

Then pardon, son. It's natural
that we should sin, being human.   615

Hippolytus

Women! This coin which men find counterfeit!
Why, why, Lord Zeus, did you put them in the world,
in the light of the sun? If you were so determined
to breed the race of man, the source of it
should not have been women. Men might have dedicated
in your own temples images of gold,   620
silver, or weight of bronze, and thus have bought
the seed of progeny, . . . to each been given
his worth in sons according to the assessment
of his gift's value. So we might have lived
in houses free of the taint of women's presence.
But now, to bring this plague into our homes   625
we drain the fortunes of our homes. In this
we have a proof how great a curse is woman.
For the father who begets her, rears her up,
must add a dowry gift to pack her off
to another's house and thus be rid of the load.
And he again that takes the cursed creature   630
rejoices and enriches his heart's jewel
with dear adornment, beauty heaped on vileness.
With lovely clothes the poor wretch tricks her out
spending the wealth that underprops his house.   635
That husband has the easiest life whose wife
is a mere nothingness, a simple fool,

uselessly sitting by the fireside.
I hate a clever woman—God forbid   640
that I should ever have a wife at home
with more than woman's wits! Lust breeds mischief
in the clever ones. The limits of their minds
deny the stupid lecherous delights.
We should not suffer servants to approach them,   645
but give them as companions voiceless beasts,
dumb, . . . but with teeth, that they might not converse,
and hear another voice in answer.
But now at home the mistress plots the mischief,
and the maid carries it abroad. So you, vile woman,   650
came here to me to bargain and to traffic
in the sanctity of my father's marriage bed.
I'll go to a running stream and pour its waters
into my ear to purge away the filth.
Shall I who cannot even hear such impurity,
and feel myself untouched, . . . shall I turn sinner?   655
Woman, know this. It is my piety saves you.
Had you not caught me off my guard and bound
my lips with an oath, by heaven I would not refrain
from telling this to my father.
Now I will go and leave this house until
Theseus returns from his foreign wanderings,
and I'll be silent. But I'll watch you close.   660
I'll walk with my father step by step and see
how you look at him, . . . you and your mistress both.
I have tasted of the daring of your infamy.
I'll know it for the future. Curses on you!
I'll hate you women, hate and hate and hate you,
and never have enough of hating. . . .
                                        Some
say that I talk of this eternally,   665
yes, but eternal, too, is woman's wickedness.
Either let someone teach them to be chaste,
or suffer me to trample on them forever.

(Phaedra comes out from behind the door. Exit Hippolytus.)

Phaedra

Bitter indeed is woman's destiny!
I have failed. What trick is there now, what cunning plea   670
to loose the knot around my neck?
I have had justice. O earth and the sunlight!
Where shall I escape from my fate?
How shall I hide my trouble?
What God or man would appear
to bear hand or part in my crime?   675
There is a limit to all suffering and I have reached it.
I am the unhappiest of women.

Chorus

Alas, mistress, all is over now   680
your servant's schemes have failed and you are ruined.

(Enter the Nurse.)

Phaedra

This is fine service you have rendered me,
corrupted, damned seducer of your friends!
May Zeus, the father of my fathers' line,
blot you out utterly, raze you from the world
with thunderbolts! Did I not see your purpose,   685
did I not say to you, "Breathe not a word of this"
which now overwhelms me with shame? But you,
you did not hold back. And therefore I must die
and die dishonored.
Enough of this. We have a new theme now.
The anger of Hippolytus is whetted.
He will tell his father all the story of your sin   690
to my disparagement. He will tell old Pittheus, too.
He will fill all the land with my dishonor.
May my curse
light upon you, on you and all the others
who eagerly help unwilling friends to ruin.

Nurse

    Mistress, you may well blame my ill-success,   695
for sorrow's bite is master of your judgment.
But I have an answer to make if you will listen.
I reared you up. I am your loyal servant.
I sought a remedy for your love's sickness,
and found, . . . not what I sought.
Had I succeeded, I had been a wise one.   700
Our wisdom varies in proportion to
our failure or achievement.

Phaedra

                So, that's enough
for me? Do I have justice if you deal me
my death blow and then say "I was wrong: I grant it."

Nurse

    We talk too long. True I was not wise then.
But even from this desperate plight, my child,   705
you can escape.

Phaedra

           You, speak no more to me.
You have given me dishonorable advice.
What you have tried has brought dishonor too.
Away with you!
Think of yourself. For me and my concerns
I will arrange all well.

                                   (Exit Nurse.)

You noble ladies of Troezen, grant me this,   710
this one request, that what you have heard here
you wrap in silence.

Chorus Leader

    I swear by holy Artemis, child of Zeus,
never to bring your troubles to the daylight.

Phaedra

    I thank you. I have found one single blessing   715
in this unhappy business, one alone,

that I can pass on to my children after me
life with an uncontaminated name,
and myself profit by the present throw
of Fortune's dice. For I will never shame you,
my Cretan home, nor will I go to face   720
Theseus, defendant on an ugly charge,
never—for one life's sake.

Chorus Leader

What is the desperate deed you mean to do,
the deed past cure?

Phaedra

                Death. But the way of it, that
is what I now must plan.

Chorus Leader

                Oh, do not speak of it!

Phaedra

No, I'll not speak of it. But on this day
when I shake off the burden of this life   725
I shall delight the Goddess who destroys me,
the Goddess Cypris.
Bitter will have been the love that conquers me,
but in my death I shall at least bring sorrow,
upon another, too, that his high heart
may know no arrogant joy at my life's shipwreck;
he will have his share in this my mortal sickness   730
and learn of chastity in moderation.

Chorus

STROPHE

Would that I were under the cliffs, in the secret hiding-places of
    the rocks,
that Zeus might change me to a winged bird
and set me among the feathered flocks.
I would rise and fly to where the sea   735
washes the Adriatic coast,
and to the waters of Eridanus.

Into that deep-blue tide,
where their father, the Sun, goes down,
the unhappy maidens weep
tears from their amber-gleaming eyes   740
in pity for Phaethon.

ANTISTROPHE

I would win my way to the coast,
apple-bearing Hesperian coast,
of which the minstrels sing.
Where the Lord of the Ocean
denies the voyager further sailing,   745
and fixes the solemn limit of Heaven
which Giant Atlas upholds.
There the streams flow with ambrosia
by Zeus's bed of love,
and holy earth, the giver of life,   750
yields to the Gods rich blessedness.

STROPHE

O Cretan ship with the white sails,
from a happy home you brought her,
my mistress over the tossing foam, over the salty sea,   755
to bless her with a marriage unblest.
Black was the omen that sped her here,
black was the omen for both her lands,
for glorious Athens and her Cretan home,
as they bound to Munychia's pier   760
the cables' ends with their twisted strands
and stepped ashore on the continent.

ANTISTROPHE

The presage of the omen was true;   765
Aphrodite has broken her spirit
with the terrible sickness of impious love.
The waves of destruction are over her head,
from the roof of her room with its marriage bed,

she is tying the twisted noose.   770
And now it is around her fair white neck!
The shame of her cruel fate has conquered.
She has chosen good name rather than life:
she is easing her heart of its bitter load of love.   775

Nurse (within)

Ho, there, help!
You who are near the palace, help!
My mistress, Theseus' wife, has hanged herself.

Chorus Leader

It is done, she is hanged in the dangling rope.
Our Queen is dead.

Nurse (within)

Quick! Someone bring a knife!   780
Help me cut the knot around her neck.

(The Chorus talks among itself.)

First Woman

What shall we do, friends? Shall we cross the threshold,
and take the Queen from the grip of the tight-drawn cords?

Second Woman

Why should we? There are servants enough within
for that. Where hands are overbusy,
there is no safety.   785

Nurse (within)

Lay her out straight, poor lady.
Bitter shall my lord find her housekeeping.

Third Woman

From what I hear, the queen is dead.
They are already laying out the corpse.

SCENE IV

(Theseus enters.)

Theseus

Women, what is this crying in the house?   790

« 265 »

I heard heavy wailing on the wind,
as it were servants, mourning. And my house
deigns me no kindly welcome, though I come
crowned with good luck from Delphi.
The doors are shut against me. Can it be
something has happened to my father. He is old.   795
His life has traveled a great journey,
but bitter would be his passing from our house.

Chorus Leader

King, it is not the old who claim your sorrow.
Young is the dead and bitterly you'll grieve.

Theseus

My children . . . has death snatched a life away?

Chorus Leader

Your children live—but sorrowfully, King.   800
Their mother is dead.

Theseus

It cannot be true, it cannot.
My wife! How could she be dead?

Chorus Leader

She herself tied the rope around her neck.

Theseus

Was it grief and numbing loneliness drove her to it,
or has there been some violence at work?

Chorus Leader

I know no more than this. I, too, came lately
to mourn for you and yours, King Theseus.   805

Theseus

Oh,
Why did I plait this coronal of leaves,
and crown my head with garlands, I the envoy
who find my journey end in misery.

(To the servants within.)

Open the doors! Unbar the fastenings,
that I may see this bitter sight, my wife
who killed me in her own death.   810

> *(The doors are opened, and Theseus goes inside. The Chorus in
> the Orchestra divide again into half-choruses and chant.)*

First Half-chorus

Woman unhappy, tortured,
your suffering, your death,
has shaken this house to its foundations.

Second Half-chorus

You were daring, you who died
in violence and guilt.
Here was a wrestling: your own hand against your life.   815

Chorus (*united*)

Who can have cast a shadow on your life?

SCENE V

(Enter Theseus.)

Theseus

O city, city! Bitterness of sorrow!
Extremest sorrow that a man can suffer!
Fate, you have ground me and my house to dust,
fate in the form of some ineffable
pollution, some grim spirit of revenge.   820
The file has whittled away my life until
it is a life no more.
I am like a swimmer that falls into a great sea:
I cannot cross this towering wave I see before me.   825

My wife! I cannot think
of anything said or done to drive you to this horrible death.
You are like a bird that has vanished out of my hand.
You have made a quick leap out of my arms
into the land of Death.

It must be the sin of some of my ancestors in the dim past 830
God in his vengeance makes me pay now.

Chorus Leader

You are not the only one, King.
Many another as well as you
has lost a noble wife. 835

Theseus

Darkness beneath the earth, darkness beneath the earth!
How good to lie there and be dead,
now that I have lost you, my dearest comrade.
Your death is no less mine. 840
Will any of you
tell me what happened?
Or does the palace keep a flock of you for nothing?

God, the pain I saw in the house!
I cannot speak of it, I cannot bear it. 845
I cannot speak of it, I cannot bear it. I am a dead man.
My house is empty and my children orphaned.
You have left them, you
my loving wife—
the best of wives 850
of all the sun looks down on or the blazing stars of the night.

Chorus

Woe for the house! Such storms of ill assail it.
My eyes are wells of tears and overrun,
and still I fear the evil that shall come. 855

Theseus

Let her be, let her be:
What is this tablet fastened to her dear hand?
What can she wish to tell me of news?
Have you written begging me to care
for our children or, in entreaty,
about another woman? Sad one, rest confident. 860
There is no woman in the world who shall come to this house

and sleep by my side.
Look, the familiar signet ring,
hers who was once my wife!
Come, I will break the seals,
and see what this letter has to tell me.   865

(The Chorus of women speak singly.)

First Woman

Surely some God
brings sorrow upon sorrow in succession.

Second Woman

The house of our lords is destroyed: it is no more.   870

Third Woman

God, if it so may be, hear my prayer.
Do not destroy this house utterly. I am a prophet:
I can see the omen of coming trouble.

Theseus

Alas, here is endless sorrow upon sorrow.
It passes speech, passes endurance.   875

Chorus Leader

What is it? Tell us if we may share the story.

Theseus

It cries aloud, this tablet, cries aloud,
and Death is its song!   880

Chorus Leader

Prelude of ruin!

Theseus

I shall no longer hold this secret prisoner
in the gates of my mouth. It is horrible,
yet I will speak.
Citizens,
Hippolytus has dared to rape my wife.   885
He has dishonored God's holy sunlight.

(He turns in the direction of the sea.)

Father Poseidon, once you gave to me
three curses. . . . Now with one of these, I pray,
kill my son. Suffer him not to escape,
this very day, if you have promised truly.   890

Chorus Leader

Call back your curses, King, call back your curses.
Else you will realize that you were wrong
another day, too late. I pray you, trust me.

Theseus

I will not. And I now make this addition:
I banish him from this land's boundaries.
So fate shall strike him, one way or the other,
either Poseidon will respect my curse,   895
and send him dead into the House of Hades,
or exiled from this land, a beggar wandering,
on foreign soil, his life shall suck the dregs
of sorrow's cup.

Chorus Leader

Here comes your son, and seasonably, King Theseus.
Give over your deadly anger. You will best   900
determine for the welfare of your house.

                    (Enter Hippolytus with companions.)

Hippolytus

I heard you crying, father, and came quickly.
I know no cause why you should mourn.
Tell me.

                    (Suddenly he sees the body of Phaedra.)

O father, father—Phaedra! Dead! She's dead!   905
I cannot believe it. But a few moments since
I left her. . . . And she is still so young.
But what could it be? How did she die, father?
I *must* hear the truth from you. You say nothing to me?   910

When you are in trouble is no time for silence
The heart that would hear everything

is proved most greedy in misfortune's hour.
You should not hide your troubles from your friends,
and, father, those who are closer than your friends.   915

Theseus

What fools men are! You work and work for nothing,
you teach ten thousand tasks to one another,
invent, discover everything. One thing only
you do not know: one thing you never hunt for—
a way to teach fools wisdom.   920

Hippolytus

Clever indeed
would be the teacher able to compel
the stupid to be wise! This is no time
for such fine logic chopping.
       I am afraid
your tongue runs wild through sorrow.

Theseus

         If there were
some token now, some mark to make the division   925
clear between friend and friend, the true and the false!
All men should have two voices, one the just voice,
and one as chance would have it. In this way
the treacherous scheming voice would be confuted   930
by the just, and we should never be deceived.

Hippolytus

Some friend has poisoned your ear with slanderous tales.
Am I suspected, then, for all my innocence?
I am amazed. I am amazed to hear
your words. They are distraught. They go indeed
far wide of the mark!   935

Theseus

The mind of man—how far will it advance?
Where will its daring impudence find limits?
If human villainy and human life

shall wax in due proportion, if the son
shall always grow in wickedness past his father,
the Gods must add another world to this   940
that all the sinners may have space enough.

Look at this man! He was my son and he
dishonors my wife's bed! By the dead's testimony
he's clearly proved the vilest, falsest wretch.   945
Come—you could stain your conscience with the impurity—
show me your face; show it to me, your father.

You are the veritable holy man!
You walked with Gods in chastity immaculate!
I'll not believe your boasts of God's companionship: 950
the Gods are not so simple nor so ignorant.
Go, boast that you eat no meat, that you have Orpheus
for your king. Read until you are demented
your great thick books whose substance is as smoke.
For I have found you out. I tell you all,   955
avoid such men as he. They hunt their prey
with holy-seeming words, but their designs
are black and ugly. "She is dead," you thought,
"and that will save me." Fool, it is chiefly that
which proves your guilt. What oath that you can swear,   960
what speech that you can make for your acquittal,
outweighs this letter of hers? You'll say, to be sure,
she was your enemy and that the bastard son
is always hateful to the legitimate line.
Your words would argue her a foolish merchant
whose stock of merchandise was her own life
if she should throw away what she held dearest
to gratify her enmity for you.   965

Or you will tell me that this frantic folly
is inborn in a woman's nature; man
is different: but I know that young men
are no more to be trusted than a woman

when love disturbs the youthful blood in them.
The very male in them will make them false.   970
But why should I debate against you in words?
Here is the dead, surest of witnesses.
Get from this land with all the speed you can
to exile—may you rot there! Never again
come to our city, God-built Athens, nor
to countries over which my spear is king.   975

If I should take this injury at your hands
and pardon you, then Sinis of the Isthmus,
whom once I killed, would vow I never killed him,
but only bragged of the deed. And Sciron's rocks
washed by the sea would call me liar when
I swore I was a terror to ill-doers.   980

Chorus Leader

I cannot say of any man: he is happy.
See here how former happiness lies uprooted!

Hippolytus

Your mind and intellect are subtle, father:
here you have a subject dressed in eloquent words;
but if you lay the matter bare of words,   985
the matter is not eloquent. I am
no man to speak with vapid, precious skill
before a mob, although among my equals
and in a narrow circle I am held
not unaccomplished in the eloquent art.
That is as it should be. The demagogue
who charms a crowd is scorned by cultured experts.
But here in this necessity I must speak.   990
First I shall take the argument you first
urged as so irrefutable and deadly.
You see the earth and air about you, father?
In all of that there lives no man more chaste
than I, though you deny it.   995

It is my rule to honor the Gods first
and then to have as friends only such men
as do no sin, nor offer wicked service,
nor will consent to sin to serve a friend
as a return for kindness. I am no railer
at my companions. Those who are my friends   1000
find me as much their friends when they are absent
as when we are together.

There is one thing that I have never done, the thing
of which you think that you convict me, father,
I am a virgin to this very day.
Save what I have heard or what I have seen in pictures,   1005
I'm ignorant of the deed. Nor do I wish
to see such things, for I've a maiden soul.
But say you disbelieve my chastity.
Then tell me how it was *your* wife seduced me:
was it because she was more beautiful
than all the other women in the world?   1010
Or did I think, when I had taken her,
to win your place and kingdom for a dowry
and live in your own house? I would have been
a fool, a senseless fool, if I had dreamed it.
Was rule so sweet? Never, I tell you, Theseus,
for the wise. A man whom power has so enchanted
must be demented. I would wish to be   1015
first in the contests of the Greeks,
but in the city I'd take second place
and an enduring happy life among
the best society who are my friends.
So one has time to work, and danger's absence
has charms above the royal diadem.   1020
But a word more and my defense is finished.
If I had one more witness to my character,
if I were tried when *she* still saw the light,
deeds would have helped you as you scanned your friends

to know the true from the false. But now I swear,
I swear to you by Zeus, the God of oaths,   1025
by this deep-rooted fundament of earth,
I never sinned against you with your wife
nor would have wished or thought of it.
If I have been a villain, may I die
unfamed, unknown, a homeless stateless beggar,
an exile! May the earth and sea refuse   1030
to give my body rest when I am dead!
Whether your wife took her own life because
she was afraid, I do not know. I may not speak
further than this.
Virtuous she was in deed, although not virtuous:
I that have virtue used it to my ruin.   1035

Chorus Leader

You have rebutted the charge enough by your oath:
it is a great pledge you took in the God's name.

Theseus

Why, here's a spell-binding magician for you!
He wrongs his father and then trusts his craft,
his smooth beguiling craft to lull my anger   1040

Hippolytus

Father, I must wonder at this in you.
If I were father now, and you were son,
I would not have banished you to exile! I
would have killed you if I thought you touched my wife.

Theseus

This speech is worthy of you: but you'll not die so.   1045
A quick death is the easiest of ends
for miserable men. No, you'll go wandering
far from your fatherland and beg your way.
This is the payment of the impious man.   1050

Hippolytus

What will you do? You will not wait until

time's pointing finger proves me innocent.
Must I go at once to banishment?

Theseus

                         Yes, and had I the power,
your place of banishment would be beyond
the limits of the world, the encircling sea
and the Atlantic Pillars.
That is the measure of my hate, my son.

Hippolytus

Pledges, oaths, and oracles—you will not test them?   1055
You will banish me from the kingdom without trial?

Theseus

This letter here is proof without lot-casting.
The ominous birds may fly above my head:
they do not trouble me.

Hippolytus

                   Eternal Gods!
Dare I speak out, since I am ruined now   1060
through loyalty to the oath I took by you?
No, he would not believe who should believe
and I should be false to my oath for nothing.

Theseus

This is more of your holy juggling!
I cannot stomach it. Away with you!
Get from this country—and go quickly!   1065

Hippolytus

Where shall I turn? What friend will take me in,
when I am banished on a charge like this?

Theseus

Doubtless some man who loves to entertain
his wife's seducers welcoming them at the hearth.

Hippolytus

That blow went home.   1070

I am near crying when I think that I
am judged to be guilty and that it is you who are judge.

Theseus

You might have sobbed and snivelled long ago,
and thought of that before when you resolved
to rape your father's wife.

Hippolytus

House, speak for me!
Take voice and bear me witness if I have sinned.   1075

Theseus

You have a clever trick of citing witnesses,
whose testimony is dumb. Here is your handiwork.

(*Points to the body.*)

It, too, can't speak—but it convicts you.

Hippolytus

If I could only find
another *me* to look me in the face
and see my tears and all that I am suffering!

Theseus

Yes, in self-worship you are certainly practiced.   1080
You are more at home there than in the other virtues,
justice, for instance, and duty toward a father.

Hippolytus

Unhappy mother mine, and bitter birth-pangs,
when you gave me to the world! I would not wish
on any of my friends a bastard's birth.

Theseus (*to the servants*)

Drag him away!
Did you not hear me, men, a long time since
proclaiming his decree of banishment?   1085

Hippolytus

Let one of them touch me at his peril! But you,
you drive me out yourself—if you have the heart!

Theseus

> I'll do it, too, unless you go at once.
> No, there is no chance that pity for your exile
> will steal on my hard heart and make me change.

> > *(Theseus goes out.)*

Hippolytus

> So, I'm condemned and there is no release.   1090
> I know the truth and dare not tell the truth.

> > *(He turns to the statue of Artemis.)*

> Daughter of Leto, dearest of the Gods to me,
> comrade and partner in the hunt, behold me,
> banished from famous Athens.
> Farewell, city! Farewell Erechtheus' land!   1095
> Troezen, farewell! So many happy times
> you knew to give a young man, growing up.
> This is the last time I shall look upon you,
> the last time I shall greet you.

> > *(To his companions.)*

> Come friends, you are of my age and of this country,
> say your farewells and set me on my way.
> You will not see a man more innocent—   1100
> innocent despite my judge!—condemned to banishment.

> > *(Hippolytus goes out.)*

Chorus

STROPHE

> The care of God for us is a great thing,
> if a man believe it at heart:
> it plucks the burden of sorrow from him.
> So I have a secret hope   1105
> of someone, a God, who is wise and plans;
> but my hopes grow dim when I see
> the deeds of men and their destinies.

> For fortune is ever veering, and the currents of life are shifting
> shifting, wandering forever.   1110

ANTISTROPHE

This is the lot in life I seek
and I pray that God may grant it me,
luck and prosperity
and a heart untroubled by anguish.
And a mind that is neither false clipped coin,
nor too clear-eyed in sincerity,   1115
that I may lightly change my ways,
my ways of today when tomorrow comes,
and so be happy all my life long.

STROPHE

My heart is no longer clear: 1120
I have seen what I never dreamed,
I have seen the brightest star of Athens,
stricken by a father's wrath,
banished to an alien land.   1125

Sands of the seashore!
Thicket of the mountain!
Where with his pacing hounds
he hunted wild beasts and killed
to the honor of holy Dictynna.   1130

ANTISTROPHE

He will never again mount his car
with its span of Venetian mares,
nor fill the ring of Limnae with the sound of horses' hoofs.
The music which never slept
on the strings of his lyre, shall be dumb,   1135
shall be dumb in his father's house.
The haunts of the Goddess Maid
in the deep rich meadow shall want their crowns.
You are banished: there's an end   1140
of the rivalry of maids for your love.

EPODE

But my sorrow shall not die,
still my eyes shall be wet with tears
for your heartless doom.
Sad mother, you bore him in vain: 1145
I am angry against the Gods.
Sister Graces, why did you let him go
guiltless, out of his native land,
out of his father's house?   1150

But here I see Hippolytus' servant,
in haste making for the house, his face sorrowful.

SCENE VI

(Enter a Messenger.)

Messenger

Where shall I go to find King Theseus, women?
If you know, tell me. Is he within doors?   1155

Chorus

Here he is coming out.

Messenger

King Theseus,
I bring you news worthy of much thought
for you and all the citizens who live
in Athens' walls and boundaries of Troezen.

Theseus

What is it? Has some still newer disaster   1160
seized my two neighboring cities?

Messenger

Hippolytus is dead: I may almost say dead:
he sees the light of day still, though the balance
that holds him in this world is slight indeed.

Theseus

Who killed him? I can guess that someone hated him,
whose wife he raped, as he did mine, his father's.   1165

Messenger

> It was the horses of his own car that killed him,
> they, and the curses of your lips,
> the curses you invoked against your son,
> and prayed the Lord of Ocean to fulfil them.

Theseus

> O Gods—Poseidon, you are then truly
> my father! You have heard my prayers.   1170
> How did he die? Tell me. How did the beam
> of Justice's dead-fall strike him, my dishonorer?

Messenger

> We were combing our horses' coats beside the sea,
> where the waves came crashing to the shore. And we were crying
> for one had come and told us that our master,   1175
> Hippolytus, should walk this land no more,
> since you had laid hard banishment upon him.
> Then he came himself down to the shore to us,
> with the same refrain of tears,
> and with him walked a countless company
> of friends and young men his own age.   1180
>
> But at last he gave over crying and said:
> Why do I rave like this? It is my father
> who has commanded and I must obey him.
> Prepare my horses, men, and harness them.
> There is no longer a city of mine.
> Then every man made haste. Before you could say the words,   1185
> there was the chariot ready before our master.
> He put his feet into the driver's rings,
> and took the reins from the rail into his hands.
> But first he folded his hands like this and prayed: 1190
> Zeus, let me die now, if I have been guilty!
> Let my father know that he has done me wrong,
> whether I live to see the day or not.
>
> With that, he took the goad and touched the horses.
> And we his servants followed our master's car,   1195

close by the horses' heads, on the straight road
that leads to Argos and to Epidaurus.
When we were entering the lonely country
the other side of the border, where the shore   1200
goes down to the Saronic Gulf, a rumbling
deep in the earth, terrible to hear,
growled like the thunder of Father Zeus.
The horses raised their heads, pricked up their ears,
and gusty fear was on us all to know,
whence came the sound. As we looked toward the shore,   1205
where the waves were beating, we saw a wave appear,
a miracle wave, lifting its crest to the sky,
so high that Sciron's coast was blotted out
from my eye's vision. And it hid the Isthmus
and the Asclepius Rock. To the shore it came,   1210
swelling, boiling, crashing, casting its surf around,
to where the chariot stood.
But at the very moment when it broke,
the wave threw up a monstrous savage bull.
Its bellowing filled the land, and the land echoed it,   1215
with shuddering emphasis. And sudden panic
fell on the horses in the car. But the master—
he was used to horses' ways—all his life long
he had been with horses—took a firm grip of the reins   1220
and lashed the ends behind his back and pulled
like a sailor at the oar. The horses bolted:
their teeth were clenched upon the fire-forged bit.
They heeded neither the driver's hand nor harness
nor the jointed car. As often as he would turn them   1225
with guiding hand to the soft sand of the shore,
the bull appeared in front to head them off,
maddening the team with terror.
But when in frenzy they charged toward the cliffs,   1230
the bull came galloping beside the rail,
silently following until he brought disaster,
capsizing the car, striking the wheel on a rock.

Then all was in confusion. Axles of wheels,
and lynch-pins flew up into the air,   1235
and he the unlucky driver, tangled in the reins,
was dragged along in an inextricable
knot, and his dear head pounded on the rocks,
his body bruised. He cried aloud and terrible
his voice rang in our ears: Stand, horses, stand!   1240
You were fed in my stables. Do not kill me!
My father's curse! His curse! Will none of you
save me? I am innocent. Save me!

Many of us had will enough, but all
were left behind in the race. Getting free of the reins,
somehow he fell. There was still life in him.   1245
But the horses vanished and that ill-omened monster,
somewhere, I know not where, in the rough cliffs.

I am only a slave in your household, King Theseus,
but I shall never be able to believe   1250
that your son was guilty, not though the tribe of women
were hanged for it, not though the weight of tablets
of a high pine of Ida, filled with writing,
accused him—for I know that he was good.

Chorus Leader

It has been fulfilled, this bitter, new disaster,   1255
for what is doomed and fated there is no quittance.

Theseus

For hatred of the sufferer I was glad
at what you told me. Still, he was my son.
As such I have reverence for him and the Gods:
I neither rejoice nor sorrow at this thing.   1260

Messenger

What is your pleasure that we do with him?
Would you have him brought to you? If I might counsel,
you would not be harsh with your son—now he is unfortunate.

Theseus

Bring him to me that I may see his face.   1265
He swore that he had never wronged my wife.
I will refute him with God's punishing stroke.

Chorus

Cypris, you guide men's hearts
and the inflexible
hearts of the Gods and with you
comes Love with the flashing wings,   1270
comes Love with the swiftest of wings.
Over the earth he flies
and the loud-echoing salt-sea.
He bewitches and maddens the heart
of the victim he swoops upon.   1275
He bewitches the race of the mountain-hunting
lions and beasts of the sea,
and all the creatures that earth feeds,
and the blazing sun sees—
and man, too—
over all you hold kingly power,   1280
Love, you are only ruler
over all these.

EPILOGUE

Artemis

I call on the noble king, the son of Aegeus,
to hear me! It is I, Artemis, child of Leto.   1285

Miserable man, what joy have you in this?
You have murdered a son, you have broken nature's laws.
Dark indeed was the conclusion
you drew from your wife's lying accusations,
but plain for all to see is the destruction
to which they led you.
There is a hell beneath the earth: haste to it,   1290
and hide your head there! Or will you take wings,

and choosing the life of a bird instead of man
keep your feet from destruction's path in which they tread?
Among good men, at least, you have no share in life.   1295
Hear me tell you, Theseus, how these things came to pass.
I shall not better them, but I will give you pain.
I have come here for this—to show you that your son's heart
was always just, so just that for his good name
he endured to die. I will show you, too,
the frenzied love that seized your wife, or I may call it,   1300
a noble innocence. For that most hated Goddess,
hated by all of us whose joy is virginity,
drove her with love's sharp prickings to desire
your son. She tried to overcome her love
with the mind's power, but at last against her will,
she fell by the nurse's strategems,   1305
the nurse, who told your son under oath her mistress loved him.
But he, just man, did not fall in with her
counsels, and even when reviled by you
refused to break the oath he had pledged.
Such was his piety. But your wife fearing
lest she be proved the sinner wrote a letter,   1310
a letter full of lies; and so she killed
your son by treachery, but she convinced you.

Theseus

Alas!

Artemis

This is a bitter story, Theseus. Stay,
hear more that you may groan the more.
You know you had three curses from your father,   1315
three, clear for you to use? One you have launched,
vile wretch, at your own son, when you might have
spent it upon an enemy. Your father,
King of the Sea, in loving kindness to you
gave you, by his bequest, all that he ought.
But you've been proved at fault both in his eyes   1320

and mine in that you did not stay for oaths
nor voice of oracles, nor gave a thought
to what time might have shown; only too quickly
you hurled the curses at your son and killed him.

Theseus

Mistress, I am destroyed.

Artemis

You have sinned indeed, but yet you may win pardon.   1325
For it was Cypris managed the thing this way
to gratify her anger against Hippolytus.
This is the settled custom of the Gods:
No one may fly in the face of another's wish:
we remain aloof and neutral. Else, I assure you,   1330
had I not feared Zeus, I never would have endured
such shame as this—my best friend among men
killed, and I could do nothing.
As for you, in the first place ignorance acquits you,
and then your wife, by her death, destroyed the proofs,   1335
the verbal proofs which might have still convinced you.
You and I are the chief sufferers, Theseus.
Misfortune for you, grief for me.
The Gods do not rejoice when pious worshippers die: 1340
the wicked we destroy, children, house and all.

Chorus

Here comes the suffering Hippolytus,
his fair young body and his golden head,
a battered wreck. O trouble of the house,
what double sorrow from the hand of God   1345
has been fulfilled for this our royal palace!

Hippolytus

A battered wreck of body! Unjust father,
and oracle unjust—this is your work.
Woe for my fate!   1350
My head is filled with shooting agony,

and in my brain there is a leaping fire.
Let me be!
For I would rest my weary frame awhile.
Curse on my team! How often have I fed you 1355
from my own hand, you who have murdered me!
O, O!
In God's name touch my wounded body gently.
Who is this standing on the right of me? 1360
Come lift me carefully, bear me easily,
a man unlucky, cursed by my own father
in bitter error. Zeus, do you see this,
see me that worshipped God in piety, 1365
me that excelled all men in chastity,
see me now go to death which gapes before me;
all my life lost, and all for nothing now
labors of piety in the face of men?

O the pain, the pain that comes upon me! 1370
Let me be, let me be, you wretches!
May death the healer come for me at last!
You kill me ten times over with this pain.
O for a spear with a keen cutting edge 1375
to shear me apart—and give me my last sleep!
Father, your deadly curse!
This evil comes from some manslaying of old, 1380
some ancient tale of murder among my kin.
But why should it strike me, who am clear of guilt?
What is there to say? How can I shake from me 1385
this pitiless pain? O death, black night of death,
resistless death, come to me now the miserable,
and give me sleep!

Artemis

Unhappy boy! You are yoked to a cruel fate.
The nobility of your soul has proved your ruin. 1390

Hippolytus

O divine fragrance! Even in my pain

I sense it, and the suffering is lightened.
The Goddess Artemis is near this place.

Artemis

She is, the dearest of the Gods to you.

Hippolytus

You see my suffering, mistress? 1395

Artemis

I see it. Heavenly law forbids my tears.

Hippolytus

Gone is your huntsman, gone your servant now.

Artemis

Yes, truly: but you die beloved by me.

Hippolytus

Gone is your groom, gone your shrine's guardian.

Artemis

Cypris, the worker of mischief, so contrived. 1400

Hippolytus

Alas, I know the Goddess who destroyed me!

Artemis

She blamed your disrespect, hated your chastity.

Hippolytus

She claimed us three as victims then, did Cypris?

Artemis

Your father, you, and me to make a third.

Hippolytus

Yes, I am sorry for my father's suffering. 1405

Artemis

Cypris deceived him by her cunning snares.

Hippolytus

O father, this is sorrow for you indeed!

Theseus

I, too, am dead now. I have no more joy in life.

Hippolytus

I sorrow for you in this more than myself.

Theseus

Would that it was I who was dying instead of you!   1410

Hippolytus

Bitter were Poseidon's gifts, my father, bitter.

Theseus

Would that they had never come into my mouth.

Hippolytus

Even without them, you would have killed me—
you were so angry.

Theseus

                    A God tripped up my judgment.

Hippolytus

O, if only men might be a curse to Gods!   1415

Artemis

Hush, that is enough! You shall not be unavenged,
Cypris shall find the angry shafts she hurled
against you for your piety and innocence
shall cost her dear.
I'll wait until she loves a mortal next time,   1420
and with this hand—with these unerring arrows
I'll punish him.

To you, unfortunate Hippolytus,
by way of compensation for these ills,
I will give the greatest honors of Troezen.
Unwedded maids before the day of marriage   1425
will cut their hair in your honor. You will reap
through the long cycle of time, a rich reward in tears.
And when young girls sing songs, they will not forget you,

your name will not be left unmentioned,
nor Phaedra's love for you remain unsung.   1430

(To Theseus.)

Son of old Aegeus, take your son
to your embrace. Draw him to you. Unknowing
you killed him. It is natural for men
to err when they are blinded by the Gods.

(To Hippolytus.)

Do not bear a grudge against your father.   1435
It was fate that you should die so.
Farewell, I must not look upon the dead.
My eye must not be polluted by the last
gaspings for breath. I see you are near this.

Hippolytus

Farewell to you, too holy maiden! Go in peace.   1440
You can lightly leave a long companionship.
You bid me end my quarrel with my father,
and I obey. In the past, too, I obeyed you.

The darkness is upon my eyes already.

Father, lay hold on me and lift me up.   1445

Theseus

Alas, what are you doing to me, my son?

Hippolytus

I am dying. I can see the gates of death.

Theseus

And so you leave me, my hands stained with murder.

Hippolytus

No, for I free you from all guilt in this.

Theseus

You will acquit me of blood guiltiness?   1450

Hippolytus

So help me Artemis of the conquering bow!

Theseus

Dear son, how noble you have proved to me!

Hippolytus

Yes, pray to heaven for such legitimate sons.

Theseus

Woe for your goodness, piety, and virtue.

Hippolytus

Farewell to you, too, father, a long farewell!   1455

Theseus

Dear son, bear up. Do not forsake me.

Hippolytus

This is the end of what I have to bear.
I'm gone. Cover my face up quickly.

Theseus

Pallas Athene's famous city,
what a man you have lost! Alas for me!   1460
Cypris, how many of your injuries
I shall remember.

Chorus

This is a common grief for all the city;
it came unlooked for. There shall be
a storm of multitudinous tears for this;
the lamentable stories of great men   1465
prevail more than of humble folk.